PLAYING THROUGH

COLLINS LIVING

An Imprint of HarperCollins *Publishers*

PLAYING
THROUGH

A Guide to the Unwritten Rules of Golf

Peter Post

HarperCollins books may be purchased for educational, business, or sales promotional use. For information please write: Special Markets Department, HarperCollins Publishers, 10 East 53rd Street, New York, NY 10022.

FIRST EDITION

Designed by Lorie Pagnozzi
Illustrations by Edwin Fotheringham

Library of Congress Cataloging-in-Publication Data
Post, Peter.
Playing through : a guide to the unwritten rules of golf / by Peter Post.—1st ed.
p. cm.
Includes index.
ISBN 978-0-06-122805-6
1. Golf—Social aspects. 2. Golfers—Conduct of life. I. Title.
GV979.S63P67 2008
796.352—dc22
2008002579

08 09 10 11 12 ID3 / RRD 10 9 8 7 6 5 4 3 2 1

ALSO FROM THE EMILY POST INSTITUTE

A Wedding Like No Other

Emily Post's Wedding Parties

Emily Post's Wedding Planner for Moms

How Do You Work This Life Thing?

"Excuse Me, But I Was Next..."

Emily Post's Wedding Planner, 4th Edition

Emily Post's Etiquette, 17th Edition

Emily Post's Wedding Etiquette, 5th Edition

Emily Post's Entertaining

Emily Post's The Etiquette Advantage in Business, 2nd Edition

Essential Manners for Couples

Essential Manners for Men

Emily Post's The Gift of Good Manners

Emily Post's The Guide to Good Manners for Kids

Emily Post's Favorite Party & Dining Tips

CONTENTS

ACKNOWLEDGMENTS

A Heartfelt Thank You . . .

First to my brothers, Allen and Bill, and to Doug, who I met on the golf course and who I play with on Thursdays and lots of other days as well. They all spent countless hours reading the manuscript, keeping me on the right path when I strayed, and honing the advice in this book. It literally could not have been done without their efforts.

To John, the professional at the Burlington Country Club (Burlington, Vermont), and to Mark, the general manager at the Edgartown Golf Club (Edgartown, Massachusetts), who responded to my questions, talked with me whenever I asked, and provided expert advice whenever I needed it.

To Katherine, our agent, for helping to make this book possible.

To Royce, who edits every piece I write, for his willingness, as a very occasional golfer, to learn the nuances of golf etiquette and to provide the beginning golfer's perspective to the advice.

To Toni at Collins for all her counsel and editing of the manuscript.

To Andy Pazder at the PGA Tour, who helped me understand the intricacies of spectator etiquette.

To the people at The Emily Post Institute for all they did to make it possible for me to concentrate on writing this book.

To Peter and Dave, who round out my regular Thursday foursome, and who have been ever so patient with me when etiquette discussions have intruded on our games. Without all those Thursdays, plus the golf outings and trips we have enjoyed over the years, this book would not have been possible.

To Bernard Magdelain for using his golf knowledge to carefully review and edit the manuscript.

To all the respondents to the Post Golf Survey. Your opinions and your stories provide the backbone of the advice here. Thank you for taking the time to respond.

To all the people, golfers and nongolfers alike, who, when they heard I was writing a book about golf etiquette, couldn't help themselves and regaled me with stories they'd heard or situations they had observed.

To Tricia, my wife, for her patience on weekends and Thursdays when I'm playing golf with the boys and for playing those wonderful, relaxing nine-hole rounds that may well be the best moments I have on the course.

INTRODUCTION

"Have I Got a Story for You!"

Whenever I explain to golfers (or to nongolfers, for that matter) that I'm writing a book about golf etiquette, invariably they reply, "Have I got a story for you!" Numerous golfers have regaled me with tales of clubs broken, or tossed into trees never to come out, or vanished to the bottom of a pond. One told me of her experience driving a cart through a bunker, while another recounted the marvelous story of two eagles being scored on the same hole by people playing in the same group. Still another described a similar situation that occurred during a tournament, when two competitors each had a hole in one on the same hole.

In order to write this book, however, I had to go outside my own experience and the stories shared by friends and acquaintances (as great as they all were), and find out exactly what it is that *really* frustrates golfers. To accomplish this, I posted a survey on The Emily Post Institute Web site explaining my project and asking golfers for their input. As it turned out, the survey respondents were no different than the people I'd been talking with in person. They offered a rich variety of both negative and positive stories about experiences they'd had and situations they'd observed on the golf course. Those stories make up much of the advice in this book. The anecdotes are all real, and they describe the actual behaviors that both impress and annoy golfers across the country on a daily basis.

The game of golf is unique, because it includes a social aspect that's found in no other sport. Before, during, and after the four-odd hours it takes to play eighteen holes, golfers are constantly interacting with their partners, their opponents, and other golfers on the course. They also rub elbows with golf course employees and other staff and members at the clubs where they play, and regularly run into other golfers in business and social settings totally apart from the course as well.

These interactions are all an integral part of the game, but they aren't codified in the USGA's *The Rules of Golf*. In other sports, the focus is clearly on the competition—not on building a relationship with your opponent at the very moment you're trying to whip him. In golf, however, the competition is only part of the story. You're certainly trying to play your best and win, but at the same time there's an equal focus on building a good relationship with the people you're playing with. In golf, how you handle yourself as you try to beat the other guy actually matters.

Over the centuries that the game of golf has been played, a number of conventions have sprung up to help guide golfers (and nongolfers). These conventions are, in fact, manners—golf manners—that clue golfers as to what to do and what to expect others to do in any situation. And there are legions of them. As with etiquette in general, golf etiquette helps the golfer navigate the tricky areas of human interaction, where making the wrong move can easily result in annoyance, ruffled feathers, or worse.

To find out just what those wrong moves are, my Web survey asked golfers to identify the top five things that frustrated them on or around the golf course, and to give examples of those frustrations. I compiled all of their answers into categories, with each category representing a key golf etiquette issue addressed in this book.

Here are the top ten, in order.

1. **SLOW PLAY.** This was by far the most-mentioned frustration.

2. **LACK OF MANNERS.** This category covers all those annoying things that golfers sometimes do—unintentionally, let's hope—ranging from showing up late for a scheduled tee time to the use of foul language on the course.

3. **TALKING AND MISUSE OF CELL PHONES.** On the golf course, there's a time to talk and a time to be quiet; but even more aggravating than a talker is the sound of a cell phone ringing during a person's backswing.

4. **NOT TAKING PROPER CARE OF THE COURSE.** This includes ball marks not fixed, divots not replaced, and littering.

5. GOLF CART ABUSE. Walking carts and riding carts are great conveniences and can save your back, but they also can wreak havoc on other people's golf games.

6. HITTING INTO OTHER GROUPS. Golf balls are hard and fly fast, and they hurt when they hit you. Golfers really don't like it when another golfer hits into them.

7. WALKING ON SOMEONE'S LINE. The green has its own particular set of manners and potential faux pas, of which walking on someone else's line is the most egregious.

8. NOT ADHERING TO THE RULES OF GOLF. The spirit of the game is embedded in knowing and following the rules, which includes being willing to call a penalty on yourself.

9. CHEATING. We all bend the rules sometimes (when we accept a gimme, for instance). But golfers really don't like playing with a cheat—and, believe me, they know who's cheating.

10. TEMPER. Throwing clubs, breaking clubs, stomping off the course—golfers are not impressed by other golfers who do these things.

I wrote this book for one reason: to help people enjoy the game of golf even more than they already do. People know there's an element of comportment to the game, but when they look for comportment advice, they hit a brick wall. There are scads of books promising to help you develop a better swing. You won't find that sort of advice here—except for one useful recommendation about putting (see Chapter 13, "To Coach or Not to Coach?" pages 132–139)—but you *will* find advice that will help you break through that brick wall. In these pages, you'll be reminded (if you're an experienced golfer) or enlightened (if you're a new golfer) about such golf behaviors as:

The importance of paying up if a wager was placed on the game—even if the person you owe is your best friend or your brother, sister, mother, or father.

The difference between friendly play and tournament play.

The difference between offering non-rules acceptable relief to an opponent in a friendly match and taking such relief yourself.

Where you should stand while others in your group tee off.

When and if you can take a mulligan—a do-over—on the tee.

When a "gimme" is acceptable.

Whether it's okay to wear jeans on the course.

Where the nineteenth hole is and what to expect there.

Trying to see how your opponent's putt is going to break by standing right behind him as he putts.

Why, unlike in basketball, where they razz the free
throw shooter unmercifully, everyone keeps quiet when
someone's hitting a golf shot.

I've often wondered what it is about my weekly Thursday
afternoon game that makes it so inviolably important to me. It
can't be the fact that I am getting better at the game, because my
handicap is rising as I get older. When I really think about it,
though, I realize that what the game gives me is a vehicle for a relaxing afternoon with three friends whose company I completely
enjoy, or an opportunity to spend a nine-hole outing of just her-
and-me time with my wife. If I stopped playing golf tomorrow,
I might not miss the duffed shots, the seven on a par 3, the infuriating four-putts, the foot-high fescue on one course I play, or
the new eyebrow traps or the monstrously difficult ninth green
(not to mention all those postage-stamp-size greens). But I would
surely miss the afternoons with my friends and those nine-hole
strolls with my wife.

Golf is about the people I get to be with and the fun I have
with them as we tackle the rigors of the course and appreciate its
challenges and its beauty. Golf etiquette—knowing what to do,
and what to expect others to do—is what helps us navigate all the
situations we find ourselves in, so that we can all enjoy the experience together. Taking the time and making the effort to respect
the etiquette—the spirit—of the game make for a better golfing
experience, more four-hour-or-less rounds, fewer three-putts,
and stronger, longer-lasting, and more-meaningful relationships
with friends and potential clients.

Golf etiquette really does matter. It's as simple as thinking before you act and asking yourself: "Is what I'm about to do really reflective of how I want others to see me?" That's what etiquette is all about. And that's what golf etiquette is all about.

PLAYING THROUGH

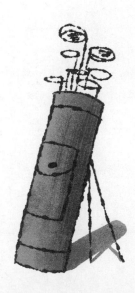

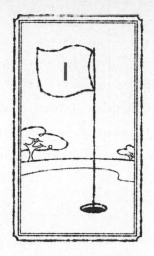

WE'RE ALL IN THIS TOGETHER

I COULD JUST AS EASILY HAVE TITLED THIS CHAPTER "SPORTSMANSHIP." Played the way it's meant to be played, golf represents the essence of sportsmanship in athletics. No other sport expects the participants to police themselves the way golf does. What's amazing to me is how, among golfers, this self-policing almost invariably leads to a reverence for following the rules.

No golfer is more legendary for his skill or his adherence to the rules of the game than the great Bobby Jones. During the play-off for the 1925 U.S. Open title at Worcester Country Club in Worcester, Massachusetts, Jones set a standard for all golfers to emulate. He was addressing his ball, which had come to rest in the rough, when he suddenly stepped away. His ball had moved. No one else had seen the movement, but he had. True to the spirit of the game, he called a two-stroke penalty on himself, then continued to play. He would finish the tournament one stroke off the lead. The two-stroke penalty he had called on himself was the margin of victory.

It didn't matter that no one else had seen that tiny movement. Jones had—and in golf, that's enough. Actions like his epitomize what has become known as "the spirit of golf." Respondents to our Post Golf Survey waxed eloquent about this spirit in all its manifestations, including:

The **sportsmanship** exemplified by the self-governing nature of the game.

The **courtesy** that golfers show each other whether they're competing for a club championship, engaging in a friendly game for "a little something," or simply playing with a regular weekly group.

The **willingness** to offer a heartfelt compliment to a competitor even as you're trying to beat him or her.

The **camaraderie** that exists between golfers.

The **beauty** of the venues where golfers play.

The **awareness** golfers have of others around them, including those within their group and those playing elsewhere on the course.

The **willingness** (and **capability**, thanks to the way the game is designed) of golfers of different abilities to play together and even enjoy some friendly competition on an equal footing.

The **respect** golfers who are strangers have for each other, including when they're paired for a round.

One survey respondent summed up the essence of the spirit of the game this way.

> **Remember the golden rule (do unto others as you would have them do unto you) in all you do, and teach this to your children and grandchildren.**

AWARENESS OF OTHERS

The golfer whom others remember fondly is the golfer who is considerate of how his actions affect others' enjoyment of the game and knows how to demonstrate this awareness. Here's a great example.

> **I was playing once in New Jersey, and a golfer in front of my group was trying to get in a round with his very young son. They had teed off far in front of our foursome, but we eventually caught up to them toward the end of the round, at which point our play slowed considerably. Still, we never managed to overtake them at a tee where we could play through. We didn't mind being held up—we thought it was cool that the young boy was out there—but his dad knew we might be getting frustrated at watching the little guy take his cuts. Just as they were coming off the eighteenth green, the beverage cart drove by them. The next thing we knew, as we were waiting to play our approach to the green, the beverage cart rolled down to us and dropped off four ice-cold beers—the father's way of thanking us for our patience.**

This book contains lots of examples of things that can go wrong on the golf course. But for every story of how golfers have been frustrated by the actions of others, there are numerous stories of the courteous things golfers do for each other, day in and day out.

One survey respondent told us how his son had made it a habit to pick up and return people's lost belongings. "I was extremely proud of my fourteen-year-old when we played golf last month. He seems to have a knack for finding people's reading glasses and other items that have fallen out of their golf carts. As we played, he kept picking up item after item as he found them, then turned them all in to the clubhouse when we'd finished the game."

Unfortunately, some golfers cringe at the sight of youngsters on a course. I can't think of a more shortsighted attitude: Golf is one of the best ways I know to instill consideration, respect, and honesty in our children. One survey respondent summed up my own feelings on this subject perfectly.

> I love the game of golf, and feel that it's the one
> sport that encourages people to be respectful of
> others. That's why I get excited to see young kids
> becoming interested in the game. I feel it teaches
> them so much more than just athletic skills. The
> game is about courtesy and manners . . . everything
> that this society is losing. Too often we don't teach
> our young people how to be respectful. Put them
> on a golf course, however, and then watch how
> totally differently they act than they do when they
> are with their peers. It's amazing.

LITTLE GESTURES THAT MEAN A LOT

As with life in general, it's often the little gestures on the part of other golfers that make people embrace golf with such passion. Here are just a few that our survey respondents cited in explaining why they love the game.

Being paired with strangers who go out of their way to be courteous, helpful, and fun to play with.

Sportsmanlike behaviors, such as when golfers compliment other golfers on their drives, putts, and form: "I'm a left-handed woman golfer who's very new to the game. I've had many experienced male golfers compliment me on my awesome southpaw swing, which I find very nice."

Golfers who pick up drinks from the beverage cart!

Anytime a golfer goes out of his way to return a club that was inadvertently left on a hole by a golfer in the group ahead of you.

Fellow golfers taking the time to pick up the other golfers' clubs on the green.

As a new golfer, being invited to play with others.

The fact that even in competition, it's okay to compliment your opponent's fantastic shot.

"I love the people who can laugh at themselves or a bad shot they made, and still enjoy the rest of the game."

Golfers who offer assistance in finding a ball that went astray.

DON'T JUDGE A BOOK BY ITS COVER

I've watched Molly grow up. She's in college now, one of the top two players on the university's women's golf team. She's always been an excellent athlete—a star soccer player, an outstanding hockey goalie (so good, in fact, that she played for the boys' team as a kid, with most of the boys several years older than she), and a rock-solid golfer. Her parents play golf as well, and it was from them that she learned her love of the game. But she couldn't always manage to play with them, and so her drive to excel led her to seek out a golf game wherever she could find it.

One of the best traditions of golf is that golfers will always make an effort to join a single with a twosome or threesome. Not only does this allow the single to play, but it also gives him or her the opportunity to meet other people with a similar passion for the game.

Molly's drive to play often led her to arrive at the first tee as a single. There she would stand and ask complete strangers if their group needed a fourth. Imagine a thirteen-year-old girl having the moxie to approach a threesome of older golfing buddies and inquire if she could join them. To their credit, despite their reservations, group after group said yes.

What they quickly discovered was that Molly was not only a good golfer who played from their tees and often outdrove and outscored them, but she was also a pleasure to be with. She fixed her ball marks and those of others, she raked the traps, she took her turn tending the flag, she knew where to stand, she knew when to talk and when to keep quiet, and she controlled her temper.

In 2006, as a college freshman, she won the Vermont State Women's Golf Association amateur championship, and in 2007 she successfully defended her title. Yet, beyond her success and skill, what makes playing with Molly a pleasure is her attitude on the course. Whether or not she makes it to the pinnacle of the pro circuit, her experience in golf will help her be a success wherever she goes and whatever she does.

GOLF: THE MEASURE OF WHO YOU ARE

Molly's real achievement isn't her handicap or her skill as a golfer—it's the way she's learned to connect with people while playing golf. Golf, more than any other sport, is really about human interaction. This is equally true whether you're playing a social round with friends or taking part in a business outing. Why is playing golf considered integral to business success? It's not because you can impress your client or your boss by beating their score. Rather, it's because the chance to observe a person on the golf course lets you quickly get a measure of what that person will be like as a client, supplier, boss, coworker, or friend. Some people mistakenly think that business literally gets conducted while playing golf. In fact, very little actual business is transacted on the course. But decisions are made and acted on after the round is completed, at the "nineteenth hole," or back at the office. Your conduct on the course definitely affects those off-course decisions. One golfer described the process this way.

> I find that the etiquette, honesty, and integrity
> of golf give me a big advantage in my business.
> I've gained nearly a dozen clients due to the
> camaraderie, integrity, and level of trust that
> players observe in the way I conduct my golf game
> (although how they pick all this up, I really don't
> know). That doesn't happen in other sports and
> situations. I've never once actually recruited or
> solicited business on the course, but clients come
> your way when you embrace the spirit of the
> game. Golf puts on display your honesty, temper,
> and ability to partner and deal with others in what
> can sometimes be stressful situations. It's a subtle
> thing, but it's painfully evident when this spirit is

not there. We all know people who don't have it on the course and, instead, are known for their dishonesty, outbursts, and rude behavior. Would you give *your* business to them?

CONSIDERATION WHEN PLAYING

One hallmark of golf is the consideration players show each other during a round. Consider the situation that confronted Jane on the tee of a par 3. Just seconds earlier, on her tee shot, she had experienced the thrill of a lifetime by notching her first ever hole in one. As the excitement died down, Katherine, her opponent, announced that she was ready to concede the hole, adding that she might as well not even bother to tee off after Jane's great shot. Jane prevailed on Katherine to step up to the tee and make her shot anyway. Lo and behold, Katherine's shot dropped into the cup on top of Jane's for a double hole in one! As a bonus, Katherine ended up halving the hole. If Jane hadn't said anything, she would have won the hole and been lauded for her accomplishment. But the spirit of golf compelled her to go the extra mile and encourage her companion, with the result that Katherine got to experience her own thrill of a lifetime, too.

THE SPIRIT OF THE GAME

As a new golfer, embrace the spirit of the game with as much vigor as you apply to learning the mechanics of the golf swing. If you do, you'll be a better, more successful, more complete golfer—and you'll enjoy the game more, too.

STOP AND SMELL THE FLOWERS

It's easy to become so wrapped up in our golf game that we forget to look around us as we're playing. Perhaps more of us should take the time to stop and appreciate the beauty of the places that, as golfers, we get to enjoy.

> I was having a particularly bad day on a course in Pagosa Springs, Colorado. After yet another lousy shot, my cart mate came over, put his hand on my shoulder, and said, "Look around." I thought he was crazy, but I did what he said and looked up anyway. It was just the most beautiful sight, with mountains and sunshine all around us. My game didn't improve much, but I didn't really care after having things put into perspective so well. No matter how bad my golf game was going, I was out in a beautiful setting, enjoying nature and friends. That's what it is all about, really.

At the moment you're attempting a shot, golf is certainly about your execution of that shot. But golf involves much more than just hitting a ball. Playing golf is about the totality of the experience. That's what keeps drawing the golfer back to the course, week after week.

PASSING THE GAME ON

Within families, the spirit of golf is often something that's handed down through the generations. Because the spirit of golf embodies life's lessons as much as it does traditions of the game, teaching golf to their children becomes an opportunity for parents to teach about life itself.

> The golf course is a place of tradition and beauty. My childhood was shaped by the lessons my father and grandfathers taught me on the links, not just about the game but about life. I always remember my dad teaching me the "real rules" of the game, such as announcing a double hit even when no one else would have seen or heard it. That's honesty, and it's how golf should be played.

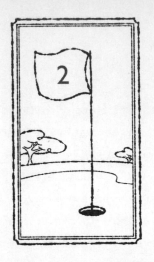

MANNERS MATTER

IMAGINE FOR A MOMENT THAT THE OFFICIAL RULE-
BOOK FOR FOOTBALL STARTED BY ESPOUSING THE
OVERRIDING PRINCIPLE OF THE GAME, WHICH IS THAT
CONSIDERATION SHOULD BE SHOWN TO THE MEMBERS
OF THE OTHER TEAM AT ALL TIMES. "Please excuse me,"
says the linebacker as he levels the quarterback with a vicious sack.
Or imagine if the NHL were to outlaw trash talking, much less
outright fighting. The very idea is laughable. Yet, not only do the
rules of golf take a stance on such etiquette issues as manners on
the course, proper respect for your opponent, and willingness to
call a penalty on yourself, but etiquette is the very first thing that
the lords of golf talk about when defining the rules of golf.

Think I'm exaggerating? Take a look at Section 1 of the
USGA's *The Rules of Golf*, and you'll see that it's titled "Etiquette:
Behavior on the Course."

Interestingly, it's not just the lords of golf who deem etiquette to be an essential part of the sport. Golfers everywhere revere the importance of manners, and are quite vocal about their frustration when a fellow golfer thumbs his nose at mannerly behavior. In fact, while our Post Golf Survey indicates that slow play is overwhelmingly the aspect of the game that golfers find most frustrating, lack of manners comes in a solid second on the list of frustrations articulated by our survey respondents. All sorts of indiscretions make up the category "Lack of Manners," but they have one thing in common: When a golfer commits one of these errors, other golfers notice the infraction and are frustrated by it. Often, manners infractions actively disrupt play and affect the other golfers' games—something they won't forget and may be hard-pressed to forgive.

RESPECT AND DISRESPECT

It would have been a drag if the only thing that people wrote about in our Post Golf Survey were all the awful things that golfers do. It really doesn't take much effort to leave a good impression that will carry over all eighteen holes and resonate long after your round is finished. Little gestures can make all the difference in how you're perceived and in the quality of the round for everyone you're playing with. Here are two examples of selfless manners at work.

> **Playing a round recently with a twosome we didn't know showed us that golf can still be a gentleman's game. The two golfers happen to play this particular course often, and they told us all about the**

course and its intricacies. They were even nice
enough to pick up our clubs on the green after we
finished putting and hand them to us. This made
the round easy and very pleasant.

I have an electric handcart. One day I hadn't
charged the battery fully and it ran out of juice.
As I was pushing it back to the clubhouse to get it
recharged, another golfer in a riding cart noticed
me, drove over, and offered to give me a lift the
rest of the way.

One Ugly Side of the Game

Unfortunately, one area where disrespect seems to rear its ugly
head is in the disturbing attitude that men can sometimes take
toward women golfers. Maybe these men think they aren't being
noticed (which is bad enough), or maybe they simply don't care
(which is worse). In fact, their disrespectful attitude *is* noticed—
and it hurts them.

A group of gentlemen at my city's country club
told my friend, who is also female, and me that we
belonged on the tennis court, not the golf course—
and then they played through our hole without
even asking if we minded.

Men, look in the mirror. If you see yourself in this story,
it's time you rechanneled your thinking. Your act isn't fooling
anyone.

THE BAD MANNERS THAT MATTER MOST

I was struck by how consistently comments to our Post Golf Survey described certain key indiscretions that golfers seem to be especially prone to repeating. Here are the most common.

Abuse of Alcohol

It's amazing how many people think they aren't affected by alcohol. The problem is, many golfers who drink alcohol while they're playing *are* affected, sometimes dramatically so. When they are, their abuse becomes a problem for other golfers. For instance:

> I played with a guy once who had been overserved on the course (actually, he brought beer with him in his golf bag) and thought it would be a good idea to do "power slides" with his golf cart. He ended up breaking the axle on his golf cart about halfway through the round, nearly flipping the cart over.

I doubt this guy started consuming beers thinking of all the fun he was going to have crashing a golf cart. Yet, crash the cart he did. That was some expensive beer! But it's not just carts that pay the price for alcohol abuse. Other golfers do, too.

> A foursome of drunks—none of whom could hit the green on a 150-yard par 3—insisted on playing from the back tees. They had the whole course backed up, and were offended when asked to move on.

Smokers Beware, Too

Ugly:

- Cigarette and cigar butts littering a course

- Ashes dumped on a green

- Smoke billowing past a golfer just as she starts to hit her shot

- Not asking if the other person sharing the cart minds before lighting up a cigar or cigarette—especially when the other person is a nonsmoker

- Taking a stance with a cigar in your mouth and suddenly smelling an acrid odor and realizing that a hole was just burned into your shirt or sweater

- A smoker standing upwind of other golfers

- Tossing a lit cigar or cigarette on the green with no concern that it could start a fire

Okay:

- Asking other golfers before lighting up

- Offering to walk while you smoke rather than riding in a cart with a nonsmoker

- Standing aside from or downwind from non-smokers

- Being careful where you flick your ashes

- Making sure your cigar or cigarette is completely out and then depositing it in a trash bin

Foul Language

Almost all of us are guilty of the occasional expletive. Asking all golfers to cease swearing, while an admirable concept, simply isn't practical. What *is* reasonable is to ask that golfers temper their language to fit the situation. Times to curb your language include:

When other golfers are nearby

When there are people in your group who could be bothered by a stream of invective

When you're playing with a stranger

In general, the occasional expletive probably won't cause any trouble. But when the swearing becomes constant and loud, even the most reasonable golfer can become annoyed.

> I recently played a round of golf with a stranger who joined our threesome. The round started out nicely enough. Our newfound fourth seemed to have a good game and could hit the ball well. He even got comfortable enough to joke around with us. After nine holes, however, his game turned. That's when the cursing began. Basically, he would swear up a storm after each shot. It got to the point where it was unpleasant to be near him.

Lateness

When one of your group is late, you have two choices: switch times with the group following you, or tee off without your buddy and have him join you on the course. Neither solution is a pleasant one. When you agree to play a round of golf, you are making a commitment to show up on time to tee off. If you're constantly late, you may find yourself out of a game altogether—and rightly so. At the very least, if you find yourself running behind, call the pro shop and ask the staff to let your group know that you'll be late, and that you'll catch up with them on the course as soon as you get there.

Relieving Yourself Obtrusively

As with so many other golf manners issues, it's not a question of whether you're going to do it, but how. Here's how *not* to do it.

> I saw a golfer unzip his pants and begin to relieve himself—in the middle of a fairway.

> I was playing golf with a guy my wife worked with— who I'd only met once before—and was attempting a putt. Immediately after hitting the putt, I looked up to see him peeing in the hole! Luckily, I missed the putt and took the next one as a gimme.

When nature calls, the preferable thing to do is wait until you're back at the clubhouse or come upon a facility on the course. If you simply can't wait, get out of view of the other golfers—behind a tree, or in the bushes—and be sure to check the sight lines not just of the golfers in your group, but also of golfers on nearby holes.

It's also important to be cognizant of the course rules wherever you're playing. Jack was golfing on a resort course where houses lined the fairways, and wasn't aware that the course had a firm "no-peeing" policy. Despite the fact that he discreetly went behind a tree to relieve himself, a homeowner spotted him in the act and reported him to the pro shop. A few minutes later, an assistant pro drove up in a cart and informed Jack of the situation. Jack had to pick up his ball and accompany the assistant back to the clubhouse, where he was then escorted out of the facility. Game over.

STILL MORE EXAMPLES OF GENERALLY OBNOXIOUS BEHAVIOR

In addition to walking on someone's line, or not fixing ball marks or divots, or throwing litter hither and yon, or welching on paying a betting debt, the bad sport is frustratingly obnoxious when he ...

- Fails to say "Thank you" when an opponent or partner says "Nice shot" or "Good putt"

- Fails to shake hands with opponent(s) and/or partner(s) at the end of a round

- Fails to watch other golfers' shots

- Fails to buy his share of the drinks after playing

- Boasts about his abilities and exclaims with pride the virtues of each shot he makes

- Finds an excuse for every poorly executed shot without ever acknowledging the real reason for his lousy play—namely, that he's simply having a bad day

STAFF DESERVE OUR RESPECT, TOO

The bag boys, the starters, the rangers, the assistants in the pro shop, the attendants in the locker room, the beverage cart person—these people are all there to make the entire golf experience go smoothly. Ask them for help or to point you in the right direction. Treat them with respect. If they go out of their way for you, consider tipping them as an appropriate way to say thank you.

The unsung heroes of course etiquette are definitely the rangers and starters who know how to properly keep players on track. They aren't highly paid, but those who do this well are the backbone of the game.

I was playing in a match, and my caddie from the club consistently helped me line up my putts—to great effect. I wish I played with her every day!

I've seen our former golf professional work hours with our junior golfers at no charge. He was a fantastic promoter of junior golf and of the game of golf in general.

Bottom line: The golf club staff members are not your servants. They deserve to be treated with the same consideration and respect you would accord anyone in the service industry.

GOOD GOLF MANNERS
THAT MATTER
Compliments—Sincere and Otherwise

Sincere compliments are great, and your opponent or your play-ing partner is sure to appreciate them. But save the accolades for when you really mean it. If, after every shot, you say, "What a great shot," it's going to get old quickly—as is your credibility.

Keeping Track of Your Ball

Mixing up your ball with someone else's is an egregious error that's irritating in the most casual of circumstances, and can be costly in a tournament or if money is on the line. At the start of each round, *take the time to mark your ball with an indelible marker.* That way, when you're looking for your ball in the rough or the bushes or the trees, you can identify it as being absolutely your ball. Even on the fairway, it's a good idea to check the ball visually to be sure it's yours before hitting it.

In tournaments, playing the wrong ball will get you into hot water fast. In match play, you lose the hole. In stroke play, you incur a two-stroke penalty; in addition, you must either go back and play your correct ball, or proceed under the rules for a lost ball or a ball in a hazard. If you fail to take one of these actions and tee off on the next hole, you will be disqualified from the event.

Correctly Marking a Ball on the Green

You're allowed to pick up your ball when it's on the green, but first you must mark its location. When marking your ball on the green, be careful how you go about it. Zoe sometimes gets a little careless when she marks her ball. She places the mark in front of her ball (between her ball and the cup), and then picks up her ball. When she replaces the ball, however, she forgets how she marked it originally, and puts the ball in front of the mark. She's just moved her ball a couple of inches closer to the hole, and broken a rule in the process.

What's the right way to mark a ball? Place your marker directly behind the ball, not in front of or to the side of it.

DON'T TOUCH MY TITLEIST!

Tom, John, and Sam are all safely on the green, while Jim is playing out of a greenside bunker. Jim's bunker shot lands on the putting surface and comes to a stop two feet in front of Sam's ball, near Sam's line. As Sam studies his upcoming putt, Tom decides to help speed up play by asking Jim, who is still climbing out of the sand trap, "Hey, Jim, would you mind if I mark your ball for you?" Jim tells him to go ahead. Then, and only then, does Tom mark Jim's ball.

WAIT UP!

In golf, order of play matters. On each hole, the person with the lowest score on the previous hole "has the honor" and hits first off the tee, the second-lowest score goes next, and so on. In a tie, whoever got the lower score on the hole *before* the previous hole goes first, and so on, going all the way back to the order of play on the first hole, if necessary.

Often this approach means that the high handicapper tees off last. The frustration for the high handicapper—which, in my group, is often me—occurs as he finishes his drive. In my case, the rest of the foursome already has their bags at the ready, and as soon as my shot flies from the tee, off they go down the fairway, enjoying each other's company, while I hurry to catch up. I've always thought that one of the best parts of golf is enjoying a pleasant conversation as you walk down the fairway. That's not possible if you're always eating your companions' dust. So a word to all you low handicappers out there: Don't be quick to push off down the fairway. Your higher-scoring buddies will thank you for it.

PUTTING TWO AND TWO (OR ONE) TOGETHER

I've been in the situation where I'm playing in a two-some with another twosome or a single playing right behind us. We see a foursome up ahead that we're going to catch on the next hole. Instead of piling up behind them—and creating that unpleas-ant dilemma where the foursome has to decide whether to let anyone through, or everyone through, or no one through—we'll invite the single or twosome to join us.

LETTING OTHER GOLFERS PLAY THROUGH

I am besieged by two conflicting emotions whenever I see a single or a twosome gaining on my foursome.

Empathy for them—based on the memory of the times I've been that single or twosome, and wished the foursome ahead of me would let me play through.

Frustration at the situation—because we're playing in a four-hour time frame. If we let them through, are we going to be faced with the same situation twenty minutes later, and again twenty minutes after that? Just how many singles and twosomes are playing behind us who could have been joined into foursomes?

Before letting any group through, I'll look ahead: Are we playing immediately behind one or more four-person groups ourselves? If we are, then letting the smaller group play through us isn't going to help them. In this situation, we'll wait until we're on the tee and they're on the green of the hole behind us, and then get their attention and explain the situation. Typically, they'll appreciate our concern and slow down a bit so that they aren't right on our tails the whole time.

If, on the other hand, we have open space in front of us, then we'll invite them through regardless of whether the group is a single, a twosome, a threesome, or a foursome. Sometimes they'll bite at the offer, and sometimes they won't. Communication coupled with a dose of consideration is the key. Besides, what goes around comes around. Who knows? Next week, *I* may be the single, and the person I just let through may be in the foursome ahead of me, and the favor will be returned.

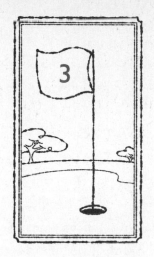

"YOU'RE OUT!" AND OTHER INTRICACIES OF GOLF ATTIRE

ON A NICE, SUNNY, HOT DAY, WOULDN'T IT BE NICE TO WEAR SHORT SHORTS, A BATHING SUIT, OR PERHAPS EVEN A BIKINI TOP OR NO TOP AT ALL?

Sure it would—just not on the golf course. While golf attire has changed over the years, a couple of things have remained constant: The clothes you wear should be *comfortable and easy to swing a club in*, and they should *keep your attention focused on the game.*

One of the simple maxims I use to teach my clients about "business casual" dress is this: "If your clothing attracts the wrong kind of attention, then it's the wrong clothing." This advice holds for golf attire as well. If I showed up to play an afternoon round in the same clothes that I'd been mucking around my garden all morning in, my partners would take notice—the wrong kind of notice. And they'd be right in doing so.

TRADITION MATTERS

Golf is a game of tradition. That tradition began hundreds of years ago, when sticks were used for clubs and stones for balls. Over the ensuing years, the specifics have changed, but the underlying success of the game still derives today—as it did centuries ago—from the ability to enjoy the company of one's friends and playing partners while still trying to put a ball into a hole in the ground in the fewest number of strokes possible. For all the bowing to tradition in our sport, however, that doesn't mean the standards for golfing attire haven't shifted with the times. For centuries, men played in knickers (or, if you were Scottish, a kilt), kneesocks, jackets, and ties, while women wore long skirts and shirts with full-length sleeves. The great Bobby Jones routinely played in knickers and a tie during his heyday in the 1920s. Today, however, ties and jackets, knickers and kneesocks, long skirts, and long-sleeved shirts are basically things of the past on golf courses in the United States. Men will still occasionally wear knickers and high socks as a tip of the hat to tradition, but a golfer showing up for a regular foursome in knickers and a tie would be an unusual sight at most clubs— private or public. (One exception was the professional golfer Payne Stewart, who made wearing knickers a signature part of his game. Seeing him dress that way really was a pleasure.)

Yes, traditions do change, even in the hallowed game of golf. And as traditions have changed, dress codes have changed as well. One issue that percolated in the early 1990s was whether golfers should be allowed to play in collarless shirts—not T-shirts, but nicely made collarless shirts. Interestingly, the tradition of wearing a collared shirt with sleeves that endured for decades has relaxed lately. Both male and female pros have recently started wearing mock tees and other collarless shirts in tournaments. But in the early 1990s, a golfer showing up to play in a sleeveless collarless shirt would have set some tongues wagging.

One of our survey respondents learned the lesson of wearing appropriate clothing from a golfing buddy who set him straight in a wise and gentle manner.

> I was playing golf once with a friend who's a great golfer. I arrived at the course in wrinkled pants and a dirty shirt. He looked at me and said, "If you want the course to respect you, you have to respect the course." To this day, whenever I play golf, I make sure that my attire shows the proper respect for the course I'm playing (although I can't say my scores always reflect mutual respect from the course).

Dressing appropriately is a matter of respect not only for the game of golf, but for the people you're playing with, for the other golfers on the course, and for the venue itself. It's not just about wearing the "right clothes"—whatever that may be for the particular venue you're playing. It's also about the condition of the clothes. Wrinkled, dirty, smelly, or torn clothing sends a message to the other people on the course that you don't respect them or the game.

PUBLIC VS. PRIVATE

Whether the courses you frequent are public or private, rules are rules. While each course may vary in its specifics, they all have regulations, including what constitutes appropriate attire. Don't assume, just because you're playing a public course, that you can show up in jeans and a T-shirt—or that you don't have to repair a divot or fix a ball mark, or that the people who play there don't care about the course's condition and reputation just as much as members of a private course care about their track. They do. And they expect you, as a guest, to care, too.

GETTING IT RIGHT

Before arriving at an unfamiliar course, check on any rules the club has for attire. You can do this by placing a quick call to the club's pro shop the day before your round, or by simply asking your host what the club's dress code is. Your host will be more than happy to oblige with the information: There's nothing worse than arriving to play a round of golf in a T-shirt and shorts, and being told that T-shirts are unacceptable and all shorts need to be Bermuda-shorts length. Fortunately, most clubs also have an assortment of clothes available in the pro shop. It would be an expensive way to rectify your mistake, but at least you could go ahead with your plans to play that day.

On the flip side, courses and clubs need to get it right, too. Draconian policies will cause golfers to flaunt the rules and push the envelope repeatedly. One survey respondent wrote in to say:

> It's really nice that many courses enforce a dress
> code. We don't need to go back to knickers and
> argyle socks, but I would like to see shorts banned.

Shorts banned? That's a bit much, I think. When committees are formulating their club's attire policies, they need to think
about what's reasonable for the golfers at that course, what's acceptable in the general golf world today, and what's enforceable
in practical terms. Their role is to strike a balance between tradition and change, and create an atmosphere that respects the golfers who play there and makes the game enjoyable for everyone.

WHEN THERE ARE NO STANDARDS

At Lisa's course, there's no dress code. So one hot sunny day, Lisa
wondered, "What's wrong with catching a few rays while playing golf?" Unfortunately for Lisa, she learned the answer to this
question firsthand.

> I was playing with my husband and another couple
> who are close friends of ours. On this day, I was
> wearing my typical outfit of shorts and a bikini top.
> Women golfing in bikini tops aren't a common
> sight at our club, but it isn't technically against the
> rules, and I'd never had a problem with it until this
> day. We had just reached the green. As we were
> studying the balls to see who should putt first, my
> female friend looked at me and said, "Lisa, you're
> out." I was perplexed, because my ball clearly was
> closer to the hole than hers. No, I replied, she was

out. We went through this a couple more times,
until finally she walked over to me and proceeded
to fix a minor wardrobe malfunction with my
bikini top.

Amazingly, once the laughter on the green
subsided, everyone in the group calmly made their
putts. The men, of course, teased me about the
incident for the rest of the round. Fortunately,
no other foursomes were nearby to witness

my malfunction—but we did run into some
acquaintances at the pro shop when we broke
for drinks between the ninth and tenth holes.
Naturally, they heard all about what had taken
place. Later, at the nineteenth hole, we learned
that they'd talked about my mishap for most of the
back nine. Apparently, the whole idea really threw
off one guy's game. Ever since then, none of us can
say the phrase "you're out" without bringing a
smile to our faces.

By the way, this incident changed my golf attire
forever.

WHAT'S APPROPRIATE TO WEAR

You've been invited to play at a local club. Perhaps your boss has
invited you. Or your future father-in-law. Or friends who are
members of the club you've applied to join. You want to make
the right impression. What do you wear?

Shirt

A golf shirt is perfect. You know the kind—a pullover shirt with
a collar and short sleeves. Usually, golf shirts will be a little longer
than an ordinary polo shirt, to help them stay tucked in even after
repeatedly swinging at the ball. Avoid loud, splashy patterns.
Keeping your look understated will keep the focus on you rather
than on your clothing.

Pants, Skirts, Skorts, and Culottes

Pants always will do very nicely—linen, khaki, cotton, or, in cold weather, wool. Unless you know they are acceptable, avoid jeans. For women, capri pants, a skirt, a skort (shorts made to look like a skirt by having a panel across the front and back), or culottes also work very nicely.

Shorts

Shorts, particularly Bermuda-length shorts, are appropriate virtually everywhere these days, especially in warm weather. Avoid gym shorts, short shorts, or cutoffs.

Shoes

Golf shoes, if you have them, are perfect. Most clubs—private or public—now require soft spikes rather than metal spikes. Your best bet is to buy a good pair of soft-spike golf shoes; then you won't have a problem at any venue. Do *not* get caught with metal spikes on a soft-spike facility—you may be asked to stop playing mid-round.

If you don't have golf shoes, a good pair of sneakers will do in a pinch. Avoid wearing street shoes with a heel, because the heel could make an impression in the green and cause a mark that could throw a putt off-line.

THE BAREFOOT GOLFER

I was giving a seminar in St. Petersburg, Florida, and suddenly found myself with a free afternoon. A couple of the participants mentioned that they were going to play a round of golf and asked if I wanted to join them. The only appropriate footwear I had was a pair of boat shoes. I rented clubs and headed for the first tee, but it quickly became apparent that my feet were slipping around in the boat shoes every time I made a swing. Somewhere around the fourth hole, I mentioned my dilemma to my companions, then removed my shoes and socks and played the rest of the round in my bare feet. I was steadier on my feet, and I didn't slip—and I couldn't believe how great the fairways and greens felt.

Would I try this at the boss's club? No. But I have seen and been in foursomes where someone has started to develop a vicious blister. Rather than suffering or leaving the course, he resorted to removing his shoes and socks and playing barefoot. With this in mind, if you're going to the boss's club to play, pack a few Band-Aids in your golf bag just in case. That way you can keep your shoes on if a blister rears its ugly head. Finally, should you choose to go barefoot someday, remember that while courses are very careful these days about what they use to improve the quality of the grass, even biofriendly fertilizers and insecticides may cause irritation to your feet.

Cool-Weather Clothes

If you play on a day that's cool or even downright cold, be prepared to layer up with a sweater, Windbreaker, and/or fleece vest or jacket, as well as any other cold-weather attire that you personally favor. When it drops below fifty degrees in Vermont, I'll still play quite happily, wearing the long underwear and hat that I also use for skiing.

Rainy-Weather Clothes

While a heavy downpour may drive you from the course, be prepared to weather a little light rain. Pants and jackets now come in water-resistant materials such as Gore-Tex that will keep you dry, but that also breathe and are supple enough to let you swing a club comfortably. Bottom line: If the forecast predicts a threat of rain, come prepared for the worst.

The Ubiquitous Golf Hat

Tony and Mark were on a golf trip. They had just settled down for a meal at a restaurant when Tony spied a fellow golfer at another table. The golfer was easy to recognize both by his clothes and by his hat, which was still on his head. Being a bit of an old-school boy, Tony asked the waiter to give the golfer a message to please take off his hat. Of course, if there isn't a specific rule for a behavior, criticizing that behavior can get very dicey. Apparently, there was no rule against wearing golf hats in the restaurant, because when the waiter carefully delivered the message on behalf of Tony, the golfer caught Tony's eye and responded with a universal salute and a carefully mouthed expletive.

The golf hat: when to doff it, and when to leave it on? The pros must get coaching about this, because they invariably handle it so gracefully. As they walk up to the eighteenth green on Sunday, they acknowledge the gallery's applause with a gracious tip of the hat. When the match is over, they never fail to take off their hats as they shake each other's hands. Nice tradition—a real show of respect for each other.

What should the rest of us do? Most assuredly, when you're in a club's dining room, follow the house rules. Many clubs have a hats-off policy indoors. If you're not sure what to do, look around: If no one else is wearing a hat, take yours off as well. If some people have hats on, take yours off anyway—especially if you're with your boss, or with members who are going to be deciding whether to admit you to the club. It's a small gesture of respect that, much like the game we all love, is steeped in tradition that goes back literally hundreds of years.

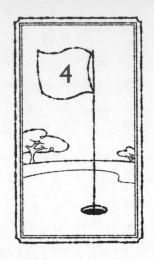

RESPECT THE COURSE

NOT ONLY IS A GOLF COURSE A LIVING THING, BUT MANY A GOLFER WILL TELL YOU THAT IT'S A SENTIENT THING, TOO. To some degree, you probably believe this yourself. Perhaps you have gotten either a lucky or unlucky bounce, then turned and proclaimed to your golfing pals: "Don't you love the home course advantage?"

Now, I'm not saying that a golf course can *intentionally* affect the bounce or roll of your golf ball. But I do believe fervently that taking care of the course makes for a better round of golf, for you and for all the other golfers at the facility—and, who knows, it might even improve your golfing karma, as well. As one survey respondent noted, "You should always fix your ball mark and two others if you can find them. . . . It's funny how many good bounces you'll get as a result."

SURVEY SAYS . . . REPAIR YOUR BALL MARKS ON THE GREEN

Of the specific course-related behaviors cited by Post Golf Survey respondents, one faux pas stands out above all others: failing to repair ball marks on the green. For the life of me, I just can't understand how a person can hit a shot onto a green, watch the ball land, and then not look for and repair the mark that the ball has just made. But they do. On any given green during any round, I can easily find three, four, or more untouched ball marks that were freshly made that day.

What makes this failure so tragic is that if a ball mark is repaired immediately after it's made, the spot quickly grows back into a smooth, unscarred stretch of grass. A ball mark left unrepaired, however, is an unfixable blemish that will remain visible for weeks. Even worse, these ball marks aren't found just on the periphery of the green. They often occur near the flagstick, where they can potentially affect the putting of every golfer playing that hole.

REPAIR MARKS OFF THE GREEN, TOO

Matt has just hit a great shot that bounces and then rolls up near the green. "Great," he thinks. "I'll putt that up close to the hole, maybe even sink it for a birdie." Dismay sets in when he arrives at his ball, however: A severe ball mark made by a previous golfer has left a crater right in front of his ball. Because Matt is off the green, the rules prohibit him from repairing that ball mark prior to hitting his next shot. Now his only option is to chip the ball onto the green—which he does, poorly. He ends up two-putting and getting a bogie instead of the hoped-for birdie.

Anytime your ball makes a mark like the one Matt encountered, take a few seconds to repair it so that it doesn't affect any player following you. Tamp it down with your club or fix it as you would a ball mark on the green (see box below).

HOW TO REPAIR A BALL MARK

Most clubs have ball-mark repair tools that they either give out as freebies or sell for a nominal fee. Carry one in your golf bag with your spare tees, ball markers, and golf glove, if you use one. To repair a ball mark:

- Insert the tool just outside the edge of the mark. Never push the tool into the mark itself.

- Press the handle of the tool forward toward the center of the mark. Repeat two or three times, moving around the mark.

- Tamp the mark gently with the sole of your putter to reestablish a smooth surface.

Do *not* insert the tool and then pull the handle away from the mark, causing the tip of the tool to lift the mark. While this may seem like an easy way to raise the indentation made by the mark, by lifting the ground you tear the roots of the grass and kill it, leaving a blemish that will take weeks to heal.

SCUFF AND SPIKE MARKS

Fixing ball marks is simple and obvious: Just do it. Dealing with other types of marks, however, is a little more complicated. The most common of these are marks made by the spikes on your golf shoes. The mark could be a simple spike-size blemish, made as you pivot on the green to walk in another direction. Or it could be a larger scuff mark, left because you don't pick up your feet as you walk across the green. I tend to make scuff marks when I'm backing away from the ball while lining up my putt. My focus is on the line, not my feet—and, as a result, a little drag of a foot can suddenly become a scuff mark.

Now, here's the rub: The rules don't allow you to repair any spike or scuff marks made by you or anyone else until *after* you've finished putting out on that hole. If someone playing ahead of you happened to leave a scuff or spike mark on the green, and it's your turn to putt and your line runs right across that scuff mark or spike mark, you wouldn't be able to repair it. Remember this the next time you and your companions have finished putting: Take the time to look at the trail you've left behind yourself on the green, then use the bottom of your putter to tamp down any spike or scuff marks so you don't leave them as a problem for the next golfer. Leaving the green in better condition than you found it—*that's* showing respect for the course.

 Business Golf Tip

Repair More Than Just Your Own Ball Mark

When playing with your boss at his golf club, be sure to look for and repair other ball marks on the green in addition to your own. Doing this fanatically on every green may be too much—but by making a reasonable effort to do so, you'll let your boss know through your actions that you respect the game and appreciate his invitation to play.

ON THE GREEN: CHIPPING AND OTHER INDISCRETIONS

When a golfer misses a putt, he wants it to be because of his own ineptitude—not because some other golfer's carelessness left a dent or gouge on the green that caused his ball to veer off-line. Here are a few other etiquette points to keep in mind when on or near the green.

No Chipping

Once in a great while, instead of putting as usual, you'll see a pro make a chip shot on the green. Technically, there's no rule that says you must use a putter on the green. However, chipping usually entails carving at least a small divot. I don't know of many amateur golfers who are so confident of their games that they could be certain not to mar the surface of the green on a chip shot. Therefore, it's best to leave this shot to the pros.

Greenside Sand Traps

It's amazing the number of things the pros do without even thinking that, frankly, we should all observe and try to emulate. Watch any golf tournament on TV, and you'll see the pro enter the sand trap, waggle his feet to get a good solid stance, and make a shot with effortless ease that lands a few feet from the pin. After a quick instinctual smoothing of the sand (his caddie does the real raking job), the pro steps out of the trap, lifts one foot, taps his shoe, lifts the other foot, taps his other shoe, and then walks to the green.

That little tapping of the shoes is a simple gesture that shows consideration for golfers in his group and those in following groups. By tapping his shoes, the golfer knocks off any sand caught on the bottom of the shoe or in the spikes. Result: no sandy footprints across the green.

The Putter Toss

Every now and then, I'll see a golfer toss a putter in the air and catch it after missing a putt. This action is *not* a good idea, for obvious reasons: Missing the catch will result in a serious gouge to the green, as well as some incredulous playing partners.

The Slammed Club

The green isn't the only place where golfers vent their anger and mar the course in the process. The most typical victim of club abuse is the tee box following a failed drive, but it also happens on the fairway, in the rough, and especially in sand traps.

The choreography goes like this: Poor shot. Magnificent slam of club. Horrific blemish on tee box. On numerous occasions, as the result of a slammed club, I've teed up my ball and taken my stance only to realize that one of my feet is in an indentation left by a frustrated golfer. When I try to ignore the problem, it ends up affecting my concentration, and I usually screw up the drive. So instead, I have to re-tee the ball and get set all over again— also causing a break in my concentration. So please: no club slamming, no matter how badly you sliced that drive.

🏌 Business Golf Tip

Be on Your Best Behavior

Here are some things to do when playing with your boss.

- Rake bunkers extra carefully, leaving them the way you found them—or even better.

- Do more than your share of putting the flag back in the hole—always being careful not to damage the edges of the hole as you do, and making sure the pin is set squarely in the hole for the next group.

- Repair any divots you create.

BUNKER ETIQUETTE: RAKE IN OR OUT?

I can never remember which way I'm supposed to leave the rake: in the bunker or out of the bunker. It seems like there's no rhyme or reason as to which standard a particular golf course uses. Frankly, I think it's left to the whim of the green's superintendents.

Different courses have different rules regarding where to leave rakes. What really matters is that you realize this, and follow the convention for the course you're on.

Raking the Bunker

The really important golf etiquette around sand traps is to use a rake to smooth the surface as you exit the trap. Goodness knows, I have enough trouble hitting out of a bunker without the added difficulty of having my ball land in the depression left by someone else's shoe or shot. The number of golfers who think they don't have any responsibility for cleaning up after themselves in a sand trap is amazing. (And no, just because your ball rolls into a depression left by some uncaring soul *doesn't* mean you get free relief.)

HOW TO REPAIR A DIVOT

If you're new to a course, check with the starter or with the golfers you're playing with regarding the best way to repair the divots *at that course*. There are two basic options.

Some courses place containers of sand mix on all golf carts and pull carts. If the course you're playing on provides a mix, simply fill the divot with the mix, then smooth the fill so it's level with the grass.

If you notice an unrepaired divot nearby, take the extra few seconds to fill it, too.

If no mix is available, retrieve the chunk of grass that came out of your divot, replace it inside the divot, and tamp down the chunk with your foot. If the displaced grass has broken into several chunks, try your best to place them in the divot in a way that leaves a smooth grass surface.

Remember that regardless of the method used, the key is to check on the correct procedure for the course you're playing, and then follow it.

FIXING DIVOTS

Let me make a quick public plea to golfers everywhere: *Fill in your divots—please!* Golf is hard enough to play without having to worry about hitting your ball out of someone else's divot. There's an inherent unfairness to hitting a great tee shot down the middle of the fairway, only to find your ball half-buried in a divot: a great shot, penalized unfairly. A number of golfers have even suggested that a rule be passed allowing them to remove their ball from a divot if it should happen to land in one. So far, the USGA has not acquiesced to their wish.

THE SHORTEST ROUTE ISN'T ALWAYS THE BEST ROUTE

For years, I've been using a pull cart (also called a pushcart) to haul my golf clubs around the course. I really never thought twice about walking between a greenside trap and the green while pulling my cart behind me. After all, what could be the problem?

Well, it turns out there *is* a potential problem with this behavior: If carts are pulled repeatedly over the same piece of ground, it can wear down the grass into a track. For this reason, my home course recently began requesting that people not roll their pull carts between the greenside bunkers and the green.

One day, after approaching the eighteenth green and blithely walking with my cart between the trap and the green, I heard a fellow member comment about how the people at the nineteenth hole were watching each group and guessing how many golfers would flaunt the rule. Needless to say, I felt a twinge of embarrassment at having been "caught." Since that day, I've stopped flaunting the rule. The rule is there for a reason. If you don't want to follow the rules at a course, don't play there.

THREE EASY STEPS TOWARD FIGHTING LITTER

- Use the waste cans. You'll find them at almost every tee.

- Stow litter in your pocket, in your golf bag, or on your cart until you can dispose of it in the next waste can.

- Go the extra mile and pick up anyone else's litter you come across.

That's showing respect for the course.

LITTER ON THE COURSE

I'm always chagrined to see litter on a golf course. A candy wrapper here, an empty POWERade bottle there: It's hard to imagine that someone intentionally throws this stuff on the ground, so I've always chosen to assume it was an accident—the golfer didn't realize the wrapper had fallen out of his pocket, or whatever. Recently, however, one of our survey respondents shattered my innocence and, at the same time, showed how a little creative aggression—in this case, for the purpose of giving an object lesson to a willful litterer—can sometimes seem acceptable.

> One day last April, three friends and I were waiting to tee off. While watching the foursome ahead of us, we observed one gentleman tossing his empty ball box into the hedges beside the tee area. We looked at one another in disbelief; then one of

us picked up the box and placed it in the trash
receptacle. When we got to the fourth hole, we
watched this same guy tossing an empty water
bottle into a line of trees. One of my friends
shouted, "What are you doing?" The litterer
responded with a universal hand signal. The final
straw came when we saw him do the water bottle
toss yet again at the eighteenth hole.

After his round, our rude friend needed a full half
hour to clean out the garbage that had somehow
made its way from the clubhouse Dumpster into
his 2001 Miata convertible sitting in the club
parking lot. He hasn't been seen at the golf course
since.

It's bad enough when you fail to respect the course and the
course returns the favor by giving you a few bad bounces. But as
this offended foursome's actions—while clearly inappropriate—
show, other golfers may also decide to take matters into their
hands if you treat their course rudely.

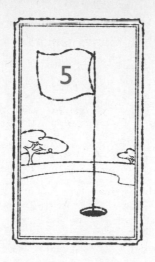

CARTS AND GREENS AND TRAPS AND WATER

GOLF CARTS HAVE A SIMPLE BUT PROFOUNDLY IMPORTANT FUNCTION: THEY LET US GET FROM THE TEE TO THE GREEN WITHOUT CARRYING OUR CLUBS. There was a time in the distant past when every golfer either carried his or her own clubs or hired a caddie to carry them. Today, while caddies still have a prominent role at certain courses (see "Why Is That Guy Taking My Clubs?" page 54), and a number of people still prefer to walk eighteen holes with their golf bag slung over their shoulder if they can, the fact is that golf carts have become a bigger and bigger part of how golfers get around the course.

Carts come in all shapes and sizes. There are handcarts, which the golfer pulls or pushes over the course. Then there are motorized handcarts—some of which come with remote-control steering. Finally, there are gas- or electric-powered riding carts.

Some courses give you the option of using a riding cart, a handcart, or no cart at all. Other courses require all golfers to use riding carts, either to generate revenue or because the distances between holes are so great as to make walking impractical.

RIDING-CART MANNERS

Regardless of why you take a cart, once you hop in, there are a few basic guidelines you'll need to follow to avoid turning your cart into one more course hazard.

Don't Fall Prey to the "Clueless Cart Driver Syndrome"

Basically, this means being aware of what's happening all around you at all times. Before you start your cart, check to be sure you won't be disturbing either the people in your own foursome or the players on adjacent holes. Primarily, you're looking for any golfers who are preparing to make a shot. The sudden noise of a cart starting or clubs banging against each other on a remote-control power cart can rattle even the most focused golfer. You also don't want to drive in front of someone as he's hitting a shot and risk getting struck by his ball.

The same holds true when you're driving along the course. Watch to be sure you aren't inadvertently disturbing other golfers. It's particularly frustrating to have a cart noisily bump past you while you're trying to hit a delicate chip shot near a green.

Your first concern should be for those playing with you, taking care that your use of the cart doesn't interfere with them as they're making a shot. As for golfers on other holes, it's really a matter of observation and judgment: If you see someone a distance away addressing the ball, you probably don't need to stop;

but if that person is nearby and your movement or noise could bother him, err on the side of caution by gently stopping your cart and waiting for him to finish the shot. Then proceed.

Avoid Driving on Tees, Traps, and Greens

To experienced golfers, this advice sounds glaringly obvious. But just because it's obvious doesn't mean people don't forget to follow it.

Crossing the Desert

When a mistake is made, it's how you recover that really matters. With a sheepish grin, Barbara told me the following story.

> **A friend and I were in a cart one day having a grand old time driving up a fairway of a course we were playing for the first time. We approached a sizable ridge, crested the top, and then realized the terrain had suddenly changed to sand. Without missing a beat, I floored the accelerator, drove right through the trap, and then screeched to a stop, all the while hoping no one had noticed. It was a harrowing surprise for both me and my passenger. We were fortunate that the cart did not flip over. Of course, we stopped, got out, and then raked the tire marks. The others in our foursome laughed about the raking being the perfect ending.**

And that is the key. The mistake was easy to make. But once made, she did the right thing: She stopped and raked the tire marks.

THE THIRTY-YARD RULE

When you're parking your golf cart in preparation for putting, how far away from the green is far enough? If you follow the thirty-yard rule—always keeping your cart at least thirty yards from the edge of the green—you'll be just right. (Usually, you'll see a cart path running alongside the green that other carts have been using. If you simply follow this, you should be okay.) By the way, the thirty-yard rule doesn't mean that you can ignore signs a hundred yards from a green directing you to the cart path.

The Shortest Distance Is a Straight Line—Even Across the Green

Driving a cart through a trap is embarrassing, to say the least. But it's not as egregious as the behavior that a friend of mine described to me recently. The perp was a relatively new golfer out for a round of golf with my friend. They were driving in a cart near a green when my friend got out to make an approach shot. Afterward, he watched in horror as the perp drove his cart right up onto the green.

Think this is a onetime event? Not so. One survey respondent reported that one of her biggest frustrations was "old guys driving their cart across the green."

> I couldn't believe my eyes! We were standing on the eighth tee and saw four older guys drive right across the seventh green in their cart! They didn't seem at all concerned—in fact, it looked like they'd done it on purpose.

BUT IF I PARK IT ON THE TEE BOX, I WON'T HAVE TO WALK AS FAR

The tee box is no different than greens or traps: Don't drive a cart onto or across it.

"It'll Never Happen to Me"

How often have you stood on the back of a golf cart, or let a walker stand on the back of your cart to get a quick lift up the fairway? Come on, it's perfectly safe—I mean, how hard is it to stand there and hold on?

Answer: harder than you think.

There's nothing like the school of hard knocks to teach you that standing on the back of a cart can be dangerous. The sixth and seventh holes at my home course are a long climb uphill toward the clubhouse. Bill and Tom had rented a cart. Doug and I were walking. After my second shot on the par-5 seventh, Bill called out to me, "Hop on—I'll drive you up to the green." As I stepped onto the back bumper, I reached forward to grab the right side of the roof. I'd done it dozens of times before—but this time I missed. Unfortunately, Bill hit the accelerator at that same instant and the cart lurched forward. As I started to fall backward, my foot slipped off the bumper. That's the last thing I remember until I woke up staring at the sky. Apparently, the cart's forward motion and my slipping foot conspired to cause my forehead to crash onto the metal frame that holds the clubs, and I was knocked senseless for about ten seconds.

I took it easy for the next couple of holes and went on to

finish the round. That night, when I lay down to go to sleep, the room started spinning. The next day, I was diagnosed with a mild concussion. The spinning stopped after a few days. I was lucky.

Bottom line: Don't ride on the back of the cart. It seems so convenient, so easy. Slip and fall? "It'll never happen to me." Until it happens to you.

PUSH-ME, PULL-YOU CARTS

Pushing or pulling a handcart is a great way to get hours of exercise without having to carry your golf bag. I used to carry my clubs on my shoulder, but nowadays, for my back's sake, I use a handcart and walk—unless the temperature is above ninety degrees, in which case I'll take a riding cart. Some clubs provide handcarts to members and guests for free, while other clubs charge a small fee. If you're at an unfamiliar facility and you're not certain what the drill is, ask the starter or someone in the pro shop before you simply take a cart. One of the backroom boys will gladly help secure your bag to the cart if you aren't sure how to do this. On this note, if you're not a regular player at the course, keep in mind the service that the backroom boys provide both in terms of helping with carts and cleaning clubs afterward: A tip is always a great way to say thank you ($5 will do nicely). If you have your own handcart, most clubs won't mind if you use it. If you're unsure about this, ask.

On the course, it's permissible to take the handcart most places where you can walk if you're carrying your bag. The obvious places not to take your handcart are across the green or through a trap. I've never seen anyone actually do this—at least not intentionally. The one way this could happen *unintentionally* is if you take the downhill-cart challenge—a challenge I've succumbed to myself. You crest a hill and find the fairway on the other side sloping away from you. As you start down the slope, you feel a slight pull on the handle; the cart wants to go faster than you're going. No problem: You line the cart up to track down the slope, and then you let go. If all works correctly, the cart will come to a satisfying stop at the bottom of the hill. Unfortunately, all doesn't always work correctly. The cart can hit a pothole, tip over on a side slope, crash into a tree (or, worse yet, another golfer), or roll into a trap, a water hazard, or across a green. Bottom line: As much fun as it may be to test your skill at aiming your cart down an incline, the best practice is to refrain from letting go.

POWERED WALKING CARTS

These devices come in two basic versions: those with remote control and those without. The no-remote-control versions have a handle or knob that turns the motor on and controls the speed. These carts are great because they let you walk the course without having to push your cart up any long or steep hills. In fact, they almost seem to help pull you up the hill. The only danger is if the cart gets away from you. This has happened to me from time to time: I've started my cart and then turned the handle a little too far while mistakenly relaxing my grip. The next thing I know, the cart is pulling away, and I have to start running to catch up with it. So far, I've never had a powered cart actually get away and run into a trap or water hazard or across a green—knock on wood.

Remote control would seem to be ideal for alleviating this problem, but experience has shown this isn't always the case. As long as the cart responds to the remote signal, all is well. But these are quirky little devices, and they don't always work as they're supposed to. My friend has a remote-control handcart, and every now and then it refuses to respond to a directional command. As the cart heads for the nearest trap, he'll point at it with the remote and push the buttons ever more frantically. So far, hitting the stop button has saved him from disaster. One day, however—as has happened to other remote-control users before him—his clubs are going to end up dumped over in a sand trap or, worse yet, soaking wet from a dunk in the water.

CONTROLLING YOUR EQUIPMENT

With any type of equipment designed to help you traverse a golf course, the key is to *be in control of it.* When you're not in control, you'll cause other golfers to lose their focus on their games—something golfers consistently cite as one of their biggest frustrations on the course.

WHY IS THAT GUY TAKING MY CLUBS?

Unfortunately, you see fewer and fewer caddies on the course these days. In times gone by, caddying was one of the great summer jobs: not only did you learn the game, but you also made a nice summer's income. Today, carts have replaced caddies at most courses. But if you do happen onto a course where there's a caddie standing ready to hoist your golf bag for you . . . *let him!*

Playing with a Caddie

When offered the opportunity to take a caddie, experienced

golfers will usually accept happily. If you're an inexperienced golfer, don't assume that caddies are only for low handicappers. If a caddie's services are offered, accept. You'll get to enjoy golf the way it was meant to be played—walking the course, appreciating the camaraderie of your fellow golfers, and enjoying the chance to get to know your caddie. Remember, many caddies are excellent golfers in their own right. Your caddie will observe and learn your skill set, help you choose which club to use on a particular shot, suggest a hoped-for line of flight for the shot, keep an eye on your ball and know where it landed, rake the trap for you, tend the pin, and help line up your putt.

On the chance that you do employ a caddie from time to time, here are a few pointers on tipping and other niceties.

Check with your host or the caddie master regarding how (and how much) the caddie is compensated.

If someone is hosting your group, the caddie's tips may be billed to the host's account or the host may choose to take care of the tips himself. Either way, always offer to cover your caddie's tip either by giving it directly to the caddie or by reimbursing your host. When there is no host, be sure to tip the caddie the customary amount directly. Tips are paid in cash and can range from $20 to $50 per bag, so come prepared by having an appropriate amount of cash in hand when you arrive at the course, in case you need it.

Always introduce yourself to your caddie; you might even let him know a little about yourself as a golfer.

Set the tone for your relationship by asking your caddie about each shot as you approach the ball: What does he estimate the distance to the hole is? Are there any obstacles you can't see? What club would he advise using? What would be a good point to aim at?

At the turn (usually, after nine holes, the course either returns you to the clubhouse or deposits you at a halfway shack), be sure to ask if your caddie would like a refreshment, such as bottled water or a soda.

When you complete your round, give your caddie his tip and thank him for his help.

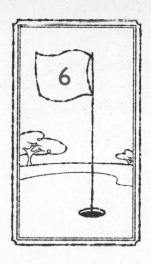

WHERE TO STAND: THE
THEORY OF THE "X"

S OME PEOPLE HAVE GREAT PERIPHERAL VISION, AND SOME DON'T. My mother obviously does. You may think you're out of her field of vision as she addresses the ball, but you're not. Suddenly, she stops and, without even looking up, says matter-of-factly, "Peter, would you mind moving out of the way?"

I thought I *was* out of the way. If I look at the situation from her point of view, however, I've broken her chain of concentration as she prepares to hit. Reasonably, she should start her shot preparation again—but in the interest of speed, she'll probably just take a deep breath and swing anyway. If it's a good shot, well done; if it's not, I'll think for sure that my standing in the wrong spot was what caused the poor shot.

It's not just my mother who's highly aware of where other

golfers stand. One female respondent added her frustration to the chorus with this observation.

> When playing with men, they always seem to stand
> behind you during your tee shots. This is soooo
> annoying. Instead of walking off their tee and going
> to the side, they stand there watching your shot.
> I feel like saying, "No need to watch for me, boys,
> I've got it. Thanks."

THINK "X"

There is a simple solution to this problem, one that all golfers should employ, regardless of whether they're on the tee box, the fairway, the rough, or the green. A fellow golfer, hearing that I was writing a book about golf etiquette, took me aside and asked if he could describe a way to solve his pet peeve: where a golfer should stand while another golfer is hitting a shot.

He sketched the solution on the back of a napkin. "Think of the person hitting as though he is standing right on the center of a big X," he said. Then he made a simple, obvious case for where it's okay to stand while a fellow golfer is hitting, and where it's not okay. In the "okay zones," be careful not to stand too close to the golfer, for his peace of mind and your safety.

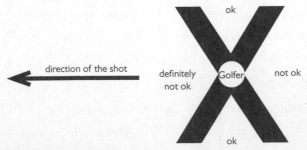

It would probably be a good idea if I use the X rule when playing with my mother. That way, I won't be in her field of vision as she's hitting.

PAUSE FOR THE CAUSE

Once a fellow golfer is addressing the ball and getting ready to hit, in addition to staying silent (see Chapter 10, "A Time to Talk and a Time to Keep Quiet," pages 106–111), you should also stop walking and stand absolutely still. It doesn't matter where you are. You may have moved ahead to greenside because your ball is already on the green, while another player is still figuring out how to hit a shot embedded in a bunker 100 yards out. Even when you're standing 100 yards away, when the other player starts to address the ball, you should *stop moving and watch*. Not only is this the considerate thing to do, but it may save you from being hit by his shot. This point was driven home for one survey respondent as he was watching his brother compete in a high school tournament.

> My brother was playing in his high school state golf tournament. His opponent would consistently walk to his next shot while my brother was still hitting. It was very, very distracting. I've noticed this behavior before in both tournament and non-tournament play. So rude!

WHAT TO DO WHEN

What should you do when someone is standing in your line of vision, or is still walking or talking nearby as you prepare to take your shot? For some reason, we think we shouldn't let these actions bother us. As a result, we often just let the matter go, even though it's affecting our shots and our enjoyment of the game. As one survey respondent observed:

> I've noticed that even people who are good golfers often have no idea where they should be standing while you're hitting. But since they're good friends, you just bite your tongue because you don't want to start an argument.

You really shouldn't let this sort of behavior go, because it *is* a distraction. Naturally, you may feel reluctant to criticize a good friend—but your need to have an atmosphere in which you can concentrate should trump any concerns about pointing out your friend's behavior. So much of success in hitting a golf ball comes from focus and concentration. Once that concentration is broken, it's hard to start over again. For this reason, the next time your concentration is interrupted, you should stop, look at the perpetrator, and ask him or her as nicely as you can: "Are you finished?" or "Do you mind . . . ?"

WHEN YOU'RE THE PERPETRATOR

If you're the person whose talking or walking is bothering a fellow golfer, don't be insulted when the golfer asks you to stop. Simply apologize, stop talking and/or walking, and try to be more aware in the future of what's going on around you and how your actions are affecting others.

IN GOLF, IT'S NOT A BALK

It's not just us everyday golfers who are affected by someone else's distracting behavior. One of the most remarkable feats of control I've seen in any sport is the ability that Tiger Woods has to stop a swing in mid-arc, even when he's already started to swing down at the ball. He'll hear a camera click or a cell phone ring, and somehow he manages to stop before he hits the ball. Unlike pitching a baseball, stopping your golf swing and starting over is not a balk, and there's no penalty for doing it—something worth remembering the next time another golfer's distracting behavior threatens to ruin one of your own shots.

LATE-SEASON SHADOWS AND OTHER DISTRACTIONS

Another factor to be especially careful of is where your shadow lands on the course—particularly in the fall, when the days get shorter and the afternoon shadows get longer earlier. One golfer described what can happen in this situation.

> I was playing with my friend John one afternoon in late autumn. After I'd teed off on the seventeenth hole, I moved twenty feet off the tee while John teed his ball up. As I was fiddling around trying to get my clubhead cover on my driver, my long fall shadow was dancing across John's ball on the tee. He gave me a look and asked if I was done yet— but in fact, we were all surprised by the length of

the shadows at that time of year, especially on the tees, where you don't normally think of this as being a problem.

Other distractions matter, too. When a fellow golfer is addressing the ball, you should be careful to refrain from:

- Rattling change in your pocket
- Removing a club from your bag or putting a club back into your bag
- Popping the top on a can of soda
- Tearing the wrapper off a candy bar
- Burping or worse

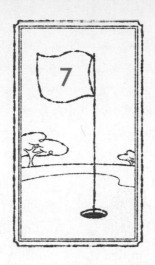

THE BIGGEST FRUSTRATION BY FAR: SLOW PLAY

T'S MY SINCERE HOPE THAT EVERYONE WHO READS THIS BOOK PICKS UP THE PACE OF THEIR GOLF GAME AS A RESULT. If they do, I like the idea of the reward proposed by one survey respondent.

> **If you can improve slow play, you deserve the Nobel Peace Prize, since this achievement is certain to provide more peace on the golf course.**

On a more serious note, the following respondent articulated the issue of slow play very clearly.

> **Slow play has got to be the biggest source**

of frustration on America's links these days.
Everywhere I play, it's an issue. The sad thing is,
even courses that employ course marshals still
can't get it right. People don't know how to be
ready when it's their turn to hit, they take too
many practice swings, and they aren't able to play
to the pace of the group in front of them.

When the Post Golf Survey asked people to list up to five behaviors that frustrate them, an astonishing two-thirds of the respondents included slow play as one of their choices. Unfortunately, it's also a problem that is often out of your control.

Example: Craig's foursome arrives a few minutes early for their 1:00 PM tee time. There on the tee, playing in the time slot just before them, is a foursome made up of host Bob Businessman and three guests. Craig's group cringes. Experience has taught them that whenever guests are involved, it usually takes longer to play a round. The guests' lack of knowledge about the course, combined with the dynamics of group socializing, make it likely that Bob's group won't finish inside four hours.

SHAVE ONE MINUTE

One minute off every hole. That's a doable, incremental saving of time that would make everyone's golf experience more pleasant. Try it the next time you play. It could be one of the most considerate things you'll ever do as a golfer.

WHAT TO DO ABOUT THE SLOWPOKES

There's no question that slow play is frustrating; but before you jump all over the group in front of you, there are a couple of things you might want to check.

WHEN ASKED TO PLAY THROUGH

Playing through is not the time to dawdle. If the group in front of you asks whether you want to play through, you'll need to:

Speed up your play. If you're on the green behind them, putt quickly; if you're not in a tournament, consider five-foot gimmes or institute a two-putt rule for that particular green.

Play super-ready golf. On the tee, have your weapon ready and hit as quickly as possible.

Walk fast to your next shot. Then, again, play super-ready golf and move on.

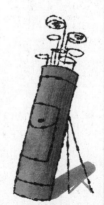

Just putt and go. If you're on a par 3 and the group that let you through is waiting for you to clear the green, again (assuming you're not playing in a tournament) opt for the two-putt rule or generous gimmes, then clear the green quickly. You don't even have to remove the pin.

Be sure to thank them. Always.

Are They Really Slow?

Maybe they *seem* slow because your group is playing fast. Before you blow a gasket, be sure they really are dawdling. You can find this out easily by checking your own elapsed time at the turn. If you've completed nine holes in two hours or less, you don't have a lot to beef about. If the group in front of you is moving along at a reasonable clip, maybe you should consider slowing down a bit. They don't deserve to have you pressing them if they're playing a four-hour round.

Are They Really the Problem?

When you encounter a slow group, before you decide to yell at them, make rude gestures, or send a missile booming over their heads, check carefully to be sure they really are the problem. What if someone else is holding *them* up? That's exactly what happened to this survey respondent.

> I had a guy in the foursome teeing off behind us scream at me to hit the ball from the fairway. I was only 210 yards from the green, however, and I thought it was only right to wait for the foursome in front of us to clear the green before I hit. The golfers on the tee hit into us, but still I held my ground and waited. After the foursome ahead of us cleared the green, I hit my second shot onto the green. I ended up making a birdie despite being harassed from the group behind me (who, by the way, never said another word to us about the speed of our play).

The Danger of Confrontation

Whether you're on the golf course, in a restaurant (see Chapter 3, " 'You're Out!' and Other Intricacies of Golf Attire," pages 25–35), or anywhere else, confronting other people about their poor behavior can result in consequences much worse than the problem itself.

> A member of a foursome that was being held up by a much slower foursome became frustrated, particularly after his group wasn't given the opportunity to play through. Fuming, he strode ahead to confront the slow players. After a few sharp words, a fistfight broke out. While I don't know the outcome, it was quite a sight to see two foursomes rolling on the fairway and swinging at each other—fortunately, without their golf clubs.

You never know how strangers will react—on or off the course—to your pointing out their poor behavior. Before you confront people, always ask yourself whether it's really worth it. If you do ask them to do something—such as speed up their play, let you play through, or stop pressing you—and they decline, be prepared to back off. It's simply not worth the possible escalation of the situation.

Defuse the Situation and Solve the Problem

When you ask the group in front of you whether you can play through, you're implicitly telling them that they're playing too slowly. So before you do this, as noted above, first make sure that they're really the problem. Anytime my foursome catches up with another group, we try to look ahead and see whether they have a hole open in front of them. If they don't, then we have to slow down.

Second, we approach them in just the way we would want to be approached if we were the slow-playing culprit. I remember being on the course recently on a beautiful, cloudless, eighty-degree day. When these days come along, you really want the outing to be perfect, even if your score isn't. Unfortunately, there was a problem: The group in front of our foursome was slow—and we were right on their tails.

Now, "slow" can mean tolerably slow, or it can mean absurdly slow. These guys were absurdly slow—they were easily headed for a five-hour round instead of the usual four hours. With every shot, we had to wait for the group ahead of us to finish before we could play. And we were only on the fourth hole!

Golf etiquette says that if one foursome is holding up another and there's an open hole in front of the slower group, the faster foursome should be invited to play through. What was frustrating in this case was that we could see there was open space ahead of them and that they knew they were playing slowly, since they kept looking back to see where we were—and yet they weren't making any motions to let us through.

What to do? Should we send a member of our group ahead as an emissary to ask if we could play through? This is an option, but it's an uncomfortable move at best. Moreover, the request can easily be turned down, which only exacerbates the situation. Finally, one of our foursome, Doug, decided to take the bull by the horns. As we were putting out on the fourth green, he approached

DON'T DO WHAT THE PROS DO

One practical piece of advice about the danger of emulating pro golfers came from a survey respondent.

This may sound a little editorial, but watching the best players in the world, either on TV or in person, and then trying to imitate them is not good for the average player. The pros are playing a game for their livelihood—something much different than our game for fun. When they take five practice swings and look at every putt from four angles, they are not setting the right example for the weekend golfer. Unfortunately, many golfers copy the pros, which results in a long day at the course. Let's keep the number of practice swings or strokes to one or two, and let's always be ready to play. Decide what you want to do and what club you're going to hit with while your playing partners are hitting their shots. Whenever you can, line up your putt while others are putting. Remember, the more enjoyable you make the game for those you're playing with, the more fun you'll have as well.

the slow group, which was preparing to tee off on the next hole. Instead of asking them if they would let us play through, he said, in the most innocent voice I've ever heard: "Would it help you if we played through?"

This was a new spin on the age-old problem of how to talk to a slow-playing group. Doug had turned the tables on them, making it appear as though we'd realized they must be uncomfortable having us playing up on them and, consequently, were going to help them out by offering to play through. By phrasing it this way, he implied that they were obviously concerned about holding us up but were unsure about how to ask us to play through. *Our* offer to play through thus became the solution to *their* problem. Doug's ploy worked to perfection. The other group motioned us forward, and we scurried to the tee, hit our drives, and moved out quickly. With clear sailing ahead, we went on to enjoy a perfect day of golf.

Just Hit the Ball, Please

One survey respondent wrote:

> **It's okay to be a bad golfer. Just be fast at it.**

Frankly, I'm not so sure it's just bad golfers who are slow. Sure, they take more whacks at the ball, and that takes up time. But numerous high-handicap golfers have pointed out that when they see faster golfers approach, they step aside. The pressure of hitting the ball is bad enough—they don't want angry eyes boring holes in the back of their heads as well.

The fact is that good golfers are slow, too—sometimes slower than bad ones. They look over their putt from every angle; they mark and clean their ball, and then, with pinpoint precision, line it up more carefully than the most meticulous pro; they pace off every shot, and take those practice swings behind the ball, and

then from the side, and then they'll look the shot over again . . .
I'm sorry. No amateur golfer—good, bad, or mediocre—is playing for the green jacket; just hit the ball and get moving, please.

Back Off and Enjoy the World Around You

My wife and I were playing a late-fall, nine-hole round at a golf
course on the Massachusetts coast. We felt like we had the course
to ourselves. It was a beautiful day: blue skies, a light wind, the
sun still warm on our backs. We weren't trying to play fast, but
on the fifth hole we started to catch up with a threesome of el-
derly gentlemen. We knew one of them, and I suspect that if we'd
shown any hint of impatience in our body language, they probably would have let us through. If they had, we might have saved
ten minutes by the end of the round.

Instead, we consciously slowed down. On the par-3 sixth,
the manager came by in a cart. He stopped, and we chatted for
a couple of minutes. On the sixth green, I looked back and saw
that the single who had been catching us had stopped play and
was headed for his car, so we took a couple of extra putts. On
this crisp fall day, the view from on top of the hill at the eighth
tee was spectacular, looking out to the ocean across a pond that
sits just behind the eighth green. As we walked down the hill to
the green, we noticed how the view changed with every step. We
were walking slowly, caught up in the beauty of the moment and
place. Before we got to the green, the threesome in front of us was
moving up the ninth hole. By the time we played nine, there was
no waiting.

The best part of all was that, after having had a triple and
a couple of doubles early on, I finished par, par, double, par, par.

That's about as good as it gets for me. Maybe slowing down and enjoying the experience helped me play better, too.

The Rules as the Culprit

Sometimes the rules butt squarely up against the desire for fast play. Example: Tony drives his ball on the twelfth tee, and it slices to the right and lands in the rough. Tony and Allen walk to where they think the ball should be, and they look and look and look. Nothing. Their five minutes are up. Now Tony has to return to the tee. After hitting another tee shot, Tony walks back up the fairway to continue play. Talk about a time waster! Including the five-minute search for the lost ball, they have just added ten to twelve minutes to their round. Meanwhile, everyone behind them is stalled. In regular, "fun" golf, the option here is to drop a ball where the lost ball disappeared and play on, counting that next shot as either your third or fourth—you decide. (If they happen to have a little wager going, then Tony is out of the hole as far as the wager is concerned.)

In tournament play, though, there's no choice: Tony *has* to go back and tee it up again. At that point, the attitude of the people behind Tony and Allen matters a lot. Fortunately for Tony, when he went back to replay his tee ball on the twelfth hole, the group waiting on the tee couldn't have been more gracious about it.

THE PROVISIONAL BALL—A GREAT TIME-SAVER

Actually, Tony had another option. When he first drove the ball, if he thought there was any chance he wouldn't be able to locate his tee shot or it might be out-of-bounds, he could have chosen to play a provisional ball before leaving the tee box. It works like this: Before hitting another tee shot, he declares to the other people in his group that this is a provisional ball, and also makes sure that it has a different marking than the first ball, so there's no confusion later. If they find the original ball—even if it's in a hazard—that is the ball in play, and he picks up the provisional ball. But if, after looking for the first ball for five minutes, he doesn't find it, the ball is lost. Tony uses his provisional ball as his ball in play. Once he plays his provisional ball, even if he then comes across his original ball, he must continue to play the provisional ball. And if he is playing his provisional ball, he is hitting his fourth shot (original drive, penalty back to the tee, and the drive with the provisional ball make three shots already).

By the way, Tony does have the option to declare the ball lost in less than five minutes, and he may want to do this if it looks like he might find it in an odious place and have to use a couple of strokes in connection with his unplayable lie, particularly if he has hit his provisional well. Even though Tony declares it lost, his partner and/or opponents are under no obligation to cease looking for the ball.

WHAT TO DO ABOUT A SLOWPOKE WITHIN YOUR FOURSOME

Unfortunately, you may sometimes be paired up with Sammy Slowpoke yourself. When that happens, not only is the resultant slow play frustrating to you, but you also end up worrying about the group waiting behind you. And besides, you really don't want to be pegged as a slow player because of someone else's actions. When stuck with Sammy, consider . . .

Making sure you and the others in your group play ready golf (see "Ready Golf—The First Line of Defense Against Slow Play," page 79). The message may become clear to Sammy once he sees the rest of his foursome hitting and moving down the fairway while he's still pacing off his shot.

Making a comment about the open space ahead. When you're on the green or on the tee, mention the open space ahead of you and then suggest that the group pick up the pace to close the gap.

Strongly suggesting to your group that you let the group behind play through. It's the least you can do if you can't speed Sammy up.

Talking directly to Sammy. "Sammy, you don't have to look at every putt from four sides. We've got at least one open hole in front of us and golfers waiting behind us. Let's pick up the pace."

Informing the starter and the pro of the problem. Let them know you did everything in your power to move Sammy along, and indicate that you don't want to be paired up with him again.

MEMORIES OF *TIN CUP*

And you thought this only happened in the movies.

We were paired up with two other golfers, one who was moderately competent and one who barely knew which end of the stick to grip. Not only couldn't the high handicapper hit the ball, but he also didn't know the first thing about golf etiquette. After suffering through seventeen holes with the better player totally ignoring his partner's ignorance of the rules of etiquette, we reached the eighteenth hole. The novice decided that since it was the final hole, for each shot he would hit balls until he got one he liked. When he'd hit more than ten shots and had only advanced about a hundred yards, we finally interceded and asked him to allow us to finish without him and his partner—which we promptly did, then hurried off to the nineteenth hole.

STRATEGIES FOR SPEEDING UP PLAY

Much of avoiding slow play in your own game is a function of being aware—really aware—of how your behavior is affecting golfers around you. I don't believe most slow play is caused intentionally. But if slow play is largely unintentional, we have a responsibility to our fellow golfers to be more conscious of our actions and to adjust them, if necessary, in order to achieve the goal of playing a four-hour round, or keeping up with the group in front of us.

With that in mind, here are some constructive suggestions on how each of us can do this better.

Offer assistance in finding a ball that went astray. Obviously, doing this for a person within your group makes sense. But sometimes this also means helping a person on an adjacent hole by pointing out where their ball landed or keeping your eye out for their ball.

Skip a hole in order to keep up with the pace of play. A novel idea, but a very effective one—especially if you want to avoid finding yourself in the position of letting one group through only to have one more right behind you.

Learn to pick up your ball, especially if you've surpassed the number of shots allowed by your handicap.

If you're learning the game or teaching someone else to play, allow others to play through. This is a time to be extra aware of others. It's also a great opportunity to teach the beginner golfer about the importance of showing courtesy on the course.

Be on time for your tee-off time. Starting late is disrespectful to your group and to the other golfers, and simply means you'll have catching up to do before you even start your round.

Observe the five-minute lost-ball rule. Remember, too, that just because you took five minutes to look for a ball doesn't mean you now have five extra minutes to finish your round. If you lost time searching for a ball, your group has a responsibility to pick up the pace and catch the group ahead or regain the four-hour-round pace. If the ball is in a thicket or some such place where it is obviously irretrievably lost, you aren't required to spend the full five minutes looking for it.

Avoid excessive practice swings. One survey respondent wrote: "I play with someone who takes at least two practice swings for each shot. By the end of the round, I just want to scream!"

Be realistic about your capabilities. If the green is 250 yards away and the best you can hit that 3-wood is 200 yards, don't wait until the group ahead of you clears the green to hit. Better yet, ask yourself why you're hitting such a low-percentage shot when a 5-iron would advance you 150 yards up the fairway, leaving a relatively easy 9-iron or pitching wedge into the green.

Encourage your club to put teeth into rules combating slow play. Write suggestions to the board of directors and the pro shop committee. If enough people complain, the board or management might actually act—but if nobody raises the issue, it almost certainly won't get dealt with.

Be ready on the green. While others are preparing to putt, look over your own putt so you can be ready to go when it's your turn.

When required to leave your cart on a cart path, take

at least a selection of clubs with you. Too often, golfers complain about the person who walks all the way across the fairway to look at their impending shot, then walks back to the cart to get a club and then back to the ball. Talk about a time waster.

Don't dawdle. Move fast enough to keep up with the group ahead of you.

Play ready golf (see box on page 79). While Short Sally is preparing to hit, Long-ball Lana can be walking toward her ball. The "X" (see Chapter 6, "Where to Stand: The Theory of the 'X,' " pages 57–62) does let Lana start moving ahead. She watches to be sure she isn't getting in Sally's way, and keeps an eye open in case Sally hits a wayward shot. Instead of talking with Sue, Lana focuses on where her ball is and what club she thinks she should use. That way, when she gets to her ball, she's ready to hit and keep moving.

Don't catch mulligan mania. The occasional mulligan (do-over) on the first tee is a nice gesture for one player to offer another. But when everyone gets in on the act, this thoughtful gesture can turn into an incredible time waster. One respondent recounted how mulligans added three-quarters of an hour to his round: "While waiting for my tee time, we watched two straight groups—all eight players—take mulligans on the first tee. Tee times were already pushed back because mulligans are a standard practice at this course. Because of this, we ended up teeing off forty-five minutes after our appointed time."

READY GOLF—THE FIRST LINE OF DEFENSE AGAINST SLOW PLAY

Before a regular Saturday game, agree to play ready golf. There's nothing more frustrating than watching one golfer arrive at his ball, select a club, practice his swing, and then, finally, make a shot—all while his three companions are standing nearby, watching him and talking. Instead of chatting, they could be moving ahead obliquely to the golfer making the shot and assessing their own next shot: what kind of shot they want to make, what club to use, where they want the ball to land. They can even reach in their bag and extract the right club. As soon as the first person has hit, they then step up to their shot, ready to swing away.

There are even times when, for the sake of speedy play, it's acceptable for a person closer to the hole to hit first. Let's say Ruth has moved ahead to her ball while Betsy is preparing to hit. Then Betsy hesitates and returns to her bag to reconsider her club selection. When Betsy steps away, Ruth, who's been ready and waiting, goes ahead and hits her shot.

Similarly, when your group is finished on the green, make the transition to the next tee as quickly and seamlessly as possible. Terry, who's last to putt, sinks his putt for a birdie, and his foursome starts for the next tee. John, who putted first and had a bogey, gets to the tee first and has his driver out. Terry calls out to John, "Go ahead—don't wait for me."

That's "ready golf." When you're ready, hit.

The twelve-minute rule. I had the pleasure once of playing in the member-guest tournament at Westchester Country Club (Rye, New York)—a great tournament on a great course (the famed West Course, I should add, is all it's cracked up to be). One of the most impressive things about the tournament was the speed of play. They had a simple rule: Your foursome had to finish no more than twelve minutes behind the foursome in front of you. A runner was stationed at the eighteenth green who immediately took your scorecard to the scorer's table for you. If you were late, you were assessed a penalty stroke on your team's best-ball score. Occasionally, an official on the course would inform you if you had fallen behind the twelve-minute time limit so you could pick up your pace. We finished in four hours each day, and it wasn't hard to do. More clubs would do well to emulate this twelve-minute rule.

THE FEARSOME FIVESOME

Slow play was just the start of this twosome's misery.

Arriving at the local course, my partner and I took off as a twosome (play was light since it was late in the morning). At the fourth hole, we encountered a fivesome. Only the starter and the pro could answer why a fivesome was allowed on the course. They did not play ready golf, nor did they make any effort to speed their play. Instead, when they got to a green, it took forever for them to putt out, since not only were there five players, but each one of them spent ages lining up their putt, pondering endlessly over the break. Repeated solicitations to play through were ignored, so we finally skipped a hole and played on. Later, the pro caught up with us, concerned that we had interrupted the flow of play by bypassing the hole. I explained that the problem was caused not by us but by the fact that a fivesome had been allowed on the course, and, more important, by the fivesome's refusal to let us play through. Unfortunately, there was no resolution, and a potentially great day of golf ended up being marred by the inconsiderate actions of the fivesome and the pro.

Occasionally, we'll end up with five of us wanting to play. Usually, that means going out as a twosome and a threesome. If the course is really empty, however, such as at the end of the season, we'll consider playing as a fivesome. Before we tee off, though, we always check with the pro. We then play an accelerated game of ready golf, and if any group does catch us, we'll move aside and let them through.

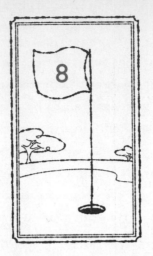

"FORE!" DOESN'T EXCUSE YOU

SHOUTING "FORE!" IS THE TRADITIONAL WAY IN WHICH GOLFERS WARN OTHER GOLFERS THAT A BALL IS HEADING THEIR WAY. So if someone yelled, "Fore," why does that guy farther down the fairway seem so mad? Because, even with a warning, it's damn scary when a ball whizzes by your head. Even worse is getting hit by one: A flying golf ball hurts like the dickens and can cause serious injury.

ATTITUDE MATTERS

It's a unique paradox of golf that when a person hits the shot of a lifetime, this unforgettably thrilling moment for her can often be a frightening experience for someone else—the person at the other end of the ball's trajectory. Suddenly, you've got two diametrically opposed emotions in play. When they interact, the result can be distinctly unfriendly.

**I happened to hit a wonderful approach shot
onto the green from two hundred yards out. It
hit just right, and rolled up into the group ahead
while they were putting. They got a little "pissy."
Thankfully, my friend was in the group on the
green and calmed them down by telling them,
"Look where she's hitting from. She hit one damn
good shot and rolled it onto the green. Get over
it!" I just grinned and went to my bag. I knew I
hadn't hit into them intentionally, and I was proud
of what I'd accomplished.**

I know how this respondent feels—proud of having hit an amazing shot. But in this kind of situation, don't wait for someone else to act as your surrogate in smoothing ruffled feathers. As she approached the green, she should have been proactively offering sincere apologies for her out-of-the-box shot. Simply grinning and walking over to her bag is not acceptable. Attitude matters.

WHAT TO DO WHEN YOU
HIT INTO A GROUP

Typically, in situations where I've seen a golfer hit into the group ahead—or when I've done it myself—the accepted practice is to yell, "Fore!" to alert them, and then wave your hand or club in the air as a gesture of apology and to signal that you're taking responsibility for having hit into them. Then, as you approach the golfers—they may be putting or perhaps on the adjacent tee—be sure to get their attention and apologize again.

Tiger Woods did this on a par 5 in the Presidents Cup

tournament in 2007. He crushed a 5-wood much farther than he'd thought he could hit it, and the ball rolled onto the green while the group ahead was still putting. Tiger apologized sincerely when he got to the green, and no ill will resulted from the incident. The way he and the group in front handled the situation was exemplary.

Just remember that if you roll it up onto a group once, as Tiger did, it's understandable—but from that point on, you'll want to be extra cautious for the rest of that round about not hitting into them a second time. Once is forgivable. Twice really will cause some trouble.

HOW TO RESPOND TO A PERSON HITTING INTO YOU

It's going to happen one day: An errant shot will roll up onto a green while you're putting, or you'll hear a thump as a ball lands close behind you, or you'll hear that hissing sound as a ball sails by your head. Adrenaline will start coursing through you, and you're going to be sorely tempted to let the perpetrator have it with both barrels. Before you do, however, take a few deep breaths and assess the situation.

How Would You Want *Your* Apology to Be Received?

Before launching into a tirade, give the other person the benefit of the doubt: It could well be that his was an amazing shot that traveled farther than he ever expected. Then give him a chance to offer an apology. Consider how *you'd* want to be treated if you hit a ball into another group by mistake. If the other person is sincerely apologetic, the best course is to accept the apology and let the situation go. If no apology is forthcoming, then you may feel compelled to pursue the matter further. Before you go on the offensive, however, take into account the fact that you can't be sure how the other person might respond. (See "Beware: Some People Don't Take Criticism Well," page 86.) If you choose to respond, you could say something like "Nice shot. Your ball's right here."

Don't Touch the Other Person's Ball

No matter how satisfying it might be, and no matter how egregious the act of hitting into you might have been, putting the offending golfer's ball on a tee or hitting it back to him or pocketing it so he ends up with a lost ball is not the answer to the problem. To repeat an old but true saying: Two wrongs don't make a right. By taking one of these actions, you risk changing the focus from the other golfer's act of hitting the ball into your group to your action in kind. Instead, keep the focus on the other person's mistake by not making a mistake yourself.

> I was in a foursome of women players playing behind a foursome of men. The club's previous pro happened to be in the men's group. One of the women hit the drive of her life, and her ball got too close to the group ahead of us. She'd yelled, "Fore," and we expected to apologize when we got the chance. Instead, the pro picked up her ball and kept it until the eighteenth hole—where he left it in the cup!! It was clear why he was the "previous" pro at that club.

Beware: Some People Don't Take Criticism Well

People tend to see rude behavior in others much more easily than they see it in themselves. In fact, when it comes to hitting into people, golfers seem to have an instantaneous knee-jerk reaction: "It's not my fault that I hit into you—it's your fault." The following respondent's story is a perfect case in point.

> My husband is just learning to play golf, so we tend to play more slowly than most. We're glad to let people play through, when appropriate. Recently, at a nice course that we hadn't played before, a group teed off into us without yelling "Fore." One tee shot bounced within two feet of our cart, and another tee shot came within a few feet of hitting me. Did they apologize? No. Instead, they proceeded to yell at us for playing too slowly.

If you hit a ball into a group ahead, no matter how egregious their play might be, and no matter how much to blame you think they are, *you* are the one at fault. Apologize.

CONSIDER ASKING A MARSHAL TO INTERCEDE

On a golf course, you may be better off letting the course marshal or his equivalent handle a sticky situation instead of interceding yourself. When the Post Golf Survey respondents took this approach (page 88), it helped them navigate difficult situations while still being able to enjoy their round of golf.

IT TAKES ALL KINDS

Unfortunately, when it comes to golf etiquette, some people are beyond help.

While playing a public course in Massachusetts, I was paired with another gentleman. As we were driving up the fairway to where our tee shots had landed, I heard a thud. My playing partner let out a terrible groan and convulsed uncontrollably. A tee shot from the hole parallel to the one we were playing had sailed off course with no warning whatsoever from Captain Hook and hit my partner directly in the gut. After uttering some expletives (not toward the wayward group, but out of sheer terror), my partner and I continued on down the hole, expecting to be met with some apologies from the adjacent group. Instead, we were met by one very angry golfer. Apparently, after his ball had attempted to perform an appendectomy on my playing partner, it had landed in front of our cart and we'd run it over. He was actually mad at us for not being more careful. He said, and I quote: "I know it hit you, but what the [bleep]! I'm playing in the club championship here."

We had these idiots behind us who kept hitting
the ball into us. At last we simply told the marshal,
who followed them for four holes. It didn't happen
again.

Playing on a very crowded course one Sunday,
we were forced to wait (as was everyone else) at
numerous tee boxes. The foursome behind us hit
into us several times, until the ranger finally kicked
them out.

PEOPLE DO THE MOST UNEXPECTED THINGS

For your own safety and that of others, whenever you're on a golf
course, you have to be very observant of other people's actions
at all times. People will do the most unexpected things—often
completely defying common sense. Don't assume *anything*. This
survey respondent did, and it led to a scary incident.

After the foursome in front of us finally finished
the hole they were playing, they got in their
cart and started to leave the area of the green.
I waited for them to go up the cart path, then
yelled, "Fore," and proceeded to hit my ball. Just
as I looked up from my follow-through, I saw that
the cart was driving straight back toward us! My
ball hit in front of them, then went between their
two carts. They then went on to scream at me for
hitting into them!

DON'T HIT NEAR A GROUP, EITHER

A ball doesn't have to actually reach you to disturb you. Occasionally, I'll be putting on a green when I hear a thump nearby. I look up, and there, a mere ten or twenty yards short of the green, is a ball hit by the group behind me. Not only is my concentration interrupted by the sound, but I can't help wondering if another ball is coming our way that will land even closer. Whenever you're in hailing distance of the people playing in front of you, give them the benefit of the doubt: If you can hit your ball ten to twenty yards behind them, you can probably reach them, too—so back off and wait until they move on before making your shot.

Why, any reasonable person might wonder, would players hit their shots, get into their cart, and then start driving the wrong way on the course? Yet it happens: Maybe they were confused; maybe they'd passed someone's ball and were going back to it; maybe they dropped a club along the way—who knows? The bottom line, however, is to be sure that the group in front of you has finished hitting and really is moving away from you before addressing your ball. A couple of seconds of careful watching could save everyone a lot of stress.

One place this sort of situation often happens to me is when people are clearing a green. The flag has been placed back in the cup, and the group in front of us starts leaving the green; I start addressing my ball, only to look up one last time to see that one of the group has turned and is walking back across the green, perhaps to pick up a club, or to retrieve his clubs that he's foolishly left on the wrong side of the green (see Chapter 9, "Around the Hole: 'Piniquette' and the Art of Watching Your Step," pages 92–105). Again, a couple of extra seconds of caution in this type of scenario can save a whole lot of grief.

BLIND SHOTS

Blind shots, in which you can't see the part of the course you're hitting to, probably account for as many instances of golfers hitting into other golfers as any other situation. It sounds ridiculously obvious to say that you should clear the area you're hitting into before launching a shot. When you're driving a car, you'd never blindly pass on a hill or a curve, would you? Instead, you wait for a place where you can see that the passing lane is clear in front of you. The same principle applies before hitting a golf shot: Make sure your landing area is clear, even if this means actually walking up and eyeballing the area yourself. When you fail to clear the area, trouble can find you quickly.

A golf ball is hard as a rock and a very dangerous missile! One time I was hit by a fellow who is one of the five best golfers at our club. He had a caddie that day, plus a cart—but neither he nor the caddie checked the green before he hit his 3-wood. He "assumed" the green was clear. Big mistake, and a very dangerous mind-set for a golfer. Said golfer had no choice regarding an apology, because I was mad as hell and had his golf ball in my hand when I confronted him by the green. He also saw how much my upper arm had already swollen at that point—my arm was double its normal size—and

that scared him. I informed him that I knew of
lawsuits that had been pursued for far less of an
injury than I had sustained. He was appropriately
humble and apologetic, and even suggested I
go to the hospital. We're still friends to this day,
but I know he'll always remember that morning
when he damn near killed someone out of sheer
stupidity and arrogance.

THE DREADED SHANK

It's not always the booming long ball that causes trouble. Severe
hooks or slices can attack people on adjacent fairways. And the
dreaded shank threatens not only people on other fairways, but
people on your own fairway, too. I've shanked the ball and damn
near clocked my partner. In fact, I know that when I have a wedge
in my hand, a full swing sometimes results in the dreaded shank.
I'm so frightened by this eventuality, in fact, that I now hit punch
shots with a 9-iron instead of a full wedge, just to guard against
it. Moral: Know your game and play safe.

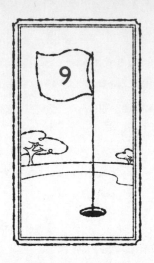

AROUND THE HOLE: "PINIQUETTE" AND THE ART OF WATCHING YOUR STEP

THE ACTUAL ACT OF PUTTING IS JUST ONE PART OF THE GAME WHEN YOU'RE ON THE GREEN. The other part involves knowing what to do and what not to do around the hole. Who putts first, how you mark your ball, who handles the flagstick—these are just a few of the many issues every golfer faces eighteen times in each round of golf. In this chapter, we'll discuss the most important greenside manners and potential missteps, including that pet peeve of golfers everywhere—walking on someone else's putting line.

STEP ONE: WATCH
WHERE YOU STEP

It's really a sign of not thinking, plain and simple. And the fact is, we're all guilty of it—at least once in a while. You get distracted, or you're analyzing your next putt, or you're listening to the latest must-hear joke. Suddenly, you're walking directly on another person's putting line. Maybe the other person says something; maybe she doesn't. But she sure does notice.

Etiquette is being aware of how your actions affect others around you. When you walk on someone's line, you don't simply add uncertainty to the putt by the fact that the ball's path could be thrown off-line by your foot's impression; you also affect the putter's state of mind. Instead of being able to focus squarely on the putt, she must now approach the putt with the added distraction of knowing that you just walked on her line. In a game where even the smallest distractions can force a mental error, you've unfairly affected the other person—simply by lack of awareness.

Here's how one survey respondent describes this "brain-freeze" syndrome.

> Only last week, in a stroke competition, a playing
> partner left his ball a foot short, so I offered to
> let him tap it in. He did so, but then proceeded to
> walk all over my line while retrieving his ball from
> the cup: just clueless.

Don't be clueless: From the minute you walk onto the green, know where your companions' balls are and where the hole is—and stay well away from the stretch of grass in between. Remember, too, that not walking on the putter's line also includes the few feet on the other side of the hole that are in line with the putt, in case the player overshoots the hole and has to putt back to the cup.

STEP TWO: HOW TO AVOID THE PUTTING LINE

Golf requires that you be observant, especially about your companions' putting lines. As soon as you reach the green, before walking to your own ball, check everyone else's ball locations to make sure that you aren't walking between another person's ball or mark and the hole, or crossing the line along which they'll likely be putting.

Sometimes you'll see a golfer take a giant step to avoid a line by stepping over it, rather than walk all the way around the line. That's okay—in fact, it may often be the best thing to do in order to keep play from slowing down.

If your ball is on a similar line but closer to the hole than the ball of one of your playing partners, approach your ball from the side rather than from behind, so you aren't stepping on the other golfer's line. You should still be sure to place your mark behind your ball, however (see "Correctly Marking a Ball on the Green," pages 21–22).

 ## Business Golf Tip

The Right Impression

The wrong impression is the one that your foot leaves on your boss's putting line. The right impression is the image of you as a thoughtful individual who is aware of how his actions affect others. Playing golf with your boss is all about image—yours. So think before you step: Look carefully to avoid walking on any other player's line.

OTHER GREENSIDE FAUX PAS

Descartes coined the saying, "I think, therefore I am." On the putting green, your fellow golfers will know for sure that "you are" every time you *fail* to think. Don't rattle change in your pocket, neglect to mark a ball, stand on someone's line, or whisper a comment just as someone is stroking a putt. A little thought about how your actions will affect others, particularly the person putting, will help ensure that everyone in your group enjoys the game. In particular, be careful of the following.

Rattling Change

It may be unconscious, but it's still *extremely* distracting to the person trying to make the putt—or any stroke, for that matter.

Standing So the Putter Is Bothered by You or Your Shadow

Peripheral vision is an amazing thing. Mine seems to get much more acute when I step onto the golf course. I've actually seen people who've committed this etiquette faux pas act as though the person putting is being much too sensitive. Wrong. As a golfer, it's your responsibility to consider how your actions will affect others—not to lecture your partners about what should and shouldn't bother them. If a playing companion complains about where you're standing, step away and watch where you stand in the future.

You'll notice that the pros are always very careful to stand a respectful distance away from the putter. If you have a putt on a very similar line to the person putting, the natural inclination is to stand behind the putter so you can see how the ball rolls. Don't. Instead, give the putter the space she deserves. If you're attentive, you'll be able to see how the ball breaks just fine from the side.

Whispering While Another Person Is Putting

Do you really think the person putting doesn't hear you?

Walking Away to the Next Tee Before Everyone Has Finished Putting

Camaraderie is one of the most important elements of golf. Part of that camaraderie involves taking an active interest in how your fellow golfers are doing. You'll never see Tiger walk off to the next tee before one of his victims has finished putting. Instead, he and the other pros show respect to the player who is putting by standing quietly greenside.

WHERE TO LEAVE YOUR BAG

Fred is just on the green. So he takes his bag off his back and places it just off the green near his ball and gets his putter. It's a long putt, all the way to the back of the green. After stroking his putt, he hurries forward to mark it so it isn't affecting the other players' putting. After everyone holes out, Fred now realizes he has to walk all the way back to the front of the green to get his bag and then scurry all the way back in the other direction across the green again to get to the next tee.

Fred had two choices: taking his bag to the back of the green before his first putt while the other players in his group were chipping on, or picking up his bag after his first putt and moving it to the back of the green. A little planning ahead speeds up play for his group and doesn't frustrate the group behind who are watching his traversing of the green while waiting to make their shots into the green.

Not Marking Your Ball

One of Bill's idiosyncrasies is that he gets distracted if another ball is left on the surface of the green while he's putting. So, even though someone else's ball on the green doesn't bother me, for his sake, I make sure to mark and remove mine whenever we're playing together. If I'm not sure whether my ball will bother another putter, rather than just leave it there, I'll ask the golfer if he'd prefer me to mark my ball.

If your ball is lying anywhere near any of your playing partners' putting lines, they have an especially good reason for wanting you to mark it: In stroke play, if you putt from on the putting surface and hit another person's ball, it's a two-stroke penalty. (In match play, there is no penalty.) In addition, you don't get a "do-over," and you don't get to place your ball where you thought it ought to go. Bottom line: If you think your putt could possibly hit another ball on the green, ask the player to mark it—and offer to mark your own if the situation is reversed.

"PINIQUETTE"

It seems like such a simple thing: The flagstick (also called the flag, pin, or stick by golfers) is there to help you see where the hole is located. Once you're on the green, however, the flag must be out of the hole when the ball drops. If it isn't and your putted ball hits the flagstick, you'll incur a two-stroke penalty in stroke play or loss of hole in match play. A simple thing, yes—but one fraught with subtle issues, as we're about to see.

Who Removes the Pin from the Hole?

Jack and Roger are part of a foursome playing in a tournament. Everyone's on the green, and it's time to start putting—but first someone needs to remove or tend the stick.

Each person is responsible for the pin during the time that he or she is putting. (If you're playing with a caddie, even though your caddie will handle the flagstick while you putt, you are still responsible if he makes a mistake.) Because the person farthest away putts first, that person is technically responsible for making sure that the stick has been removed from the cup and laid on or beside the green, or that someone is tending it and is poised to remove it as the ball approaches the hole. He's responsible because he's the one who will incur the penalty if his ball hits the flagstick. The problem with this scenario, however, is that it will slow play significantly if the person farthest away has to walk over to the cup, take the pin out of the hole, walk back to his ball, and make his putt.

Golfers typically get around this issue by sharing pin duty. For instance, a group may have an unwritten rule that whoever is closest to the hole handles the flagstick. Here's how it works: In Jack and Roger's group, Roger is farthest from the hole and Jack is closest. While Roger is lining up his putt and addressing the ball, Jack steps to the flagstick and lightly holds it. He may even ask, "Hey, Roger, would you like me to tend it or remove it?"

With a simple "Tend it for me, please. Thank you!" Roger is appropriately appreciative of Jack's offer.

The Etiquette of Tending the Flagstick

If the person removing the flag doesn't offer to tend it, it's perfectly okay for the putter to request that he do so: "Jack, would you mind tending the pin for me on this one? Thanks!" When Jack moves to the pin to tend it, he's conscious of several things.

> He looks at where all the players' balls and/or marks are and makes sure he isn't standing in or near someone's line.

He checks Roger's line and stands to the opposite side of the pin from Roger's probable line. That way he doesn't give Roger something like his right foot to aim his putt at.

He jiggles the flagstick to make sure it is loose, or he actually removes the end of the pin from the socket in the hole in order to be sure he can easily pull the flag out before Roger's putt gets to the hole.

He makes sure his shadow isn't falling across either the hole or Roger's probable putting line.

He holds the flag as well as the stick, to keep the flag from fluttering in a breeze.

More about Tending the Pin

If Jack is tending the pin, it's important that he not be daydreaming and gazing at the beautiful scenery instead of paying attention to what's happening on the green. Roger isn't worried about hitting the flagstick, because Jack has agreed to tend it. Roger lines up his putt and lets it go. Just then, Jack notices a beautiful red-tailed hawk swoop down and grab an unsuspecting mouse. At the same instant, Roger's ball hits the stick and drops into the hole. Instead of being excited that he holed the putt, Roger will be annoyed by the two-stroke penalty he just incurred for hitting the flagstick.

LET'S GET REAL

If you're playing with someone who's a stickler for a particular point of golf etiquette—if, for instance, he can't stand it when anyone touches a pin that's been placed on the ground before everyone has finished putting—don't touch the pin. In this type of situation, follow the path of least resistance. It'll keep you from getting into an argument, and make the round more tolerable for everyone involved. You'll play better if you're calm and focused, as opposed to being angry and frustrated. Make a big deal about something that really matters; getting upset over this sort of nitpicking isn't worth it.

Where to Put the Flagstick Down

If everyone in your group has reasonably short putts, the usual approach prior to putting is to take the pin out of the cup and lay it down in an unobtrusive spot. Most players will tell you that the best place to put a flagstick after removing it from the cup is on the fringe of the green, rather than on the putting surface itself. Even if you're placing the pin off the surface of the green, however, you should still be conscious of the lines of your group's putts, and avoid placing the pin directly near anyone's line. Be careful not to place the pin anywhere near where a person's putt might hit it. Place the pin down on the ground gently—never drop it. If you have a potentially bad back, as I do, try this trick:

Rest one end of the pin on the top of your putter's head, then use the putter to gently lower it to the ground.

Holding the Stick

Wanting to be proactive about avoiding slow play, you decide to pick the flag up from where it was lying so you'll be ready to re-place it in the hole as soon as Mary, the last person to putt, ad-dresses her ball. Just then, the breeze picks up, the flag starts flut-tering, and Mary yips her putt. She glares at you, since clearly it's your fault and not hers that she missed the putt.

Want to drive someone nuts? Let the flag flutter in the breeze as you hold the pin. Want to preserve the peace? Hold the flag itself along with the pin, or hold the pin upside down with your foot on the flag. Also, remember to stand absolutely still so that whoever is putting can concentrate on his or her putt.

JUST WHEN I THOUGHT I'D HEARD IT ALL . . .

One of our Post Golf Survey respondents told the following story.

We were playing with another couple at our club one night, and the woman playing with us wasn't putting very well. Finally, on one hole, she walked up to the cup and stamped down the turf around the hole so it would make a sort of funnel into the cup. My husband and I were horrified. The woman sank her putt—as did we all. She's an older widow and was partnered that evening with another man from our club, who didn't really say anything other than to jokingly chide her. We didn't say anything either, since we'd just joined the club and she's been a club member for years and years. Fortunately, this was one of our last holes, and she didn't repeat the action—at least, not on that day.

Not only does that woman need to be taught some golf etiquette, but she also should have been assessed a two-stroke penalty in stroke play (or loss of the hole in match play).

Replacing the Pin

The convention my golfing partners and I play by is this: The second-to-last player to finish putting replaces the pin, unless the final putter volunteers to get it. Meanwhile, the first two people to

finish putting position themselves on the edge of the green nearest the tee for the next hole, so that they can quickly step to the tee
and prepare to drive. This approach helps combat slow play (see
Chapter 7, "The Biggest Frustration by Far: Slow Play," pages
63–81).

Two caveats to having the first two putters move to the edge
of the green in order to be ready to move to the next hole: First,
it's important that they stay by the edge of the green and watch
the last person finish putting out before moving to the next hole.
Second, the order in which a group hits off the tee matters. Usually, the person with the lowest score on the previous hole tees off
first. But if that person happens to be the last person putting and
is slow getting to the next tee, he should inform those already on
the tee to go ahead and hit, even though this means they'll be hitting out of order.

PROTECTING THE CUP

Be careful of the cup whenever you're removing or replacing the
pin. A gouge made in the ground around the cup while replacing the pin should be repaired as best you can by smoothing it
out with a ball-mark repair tool or the bottom of your putter.
Similarly, if your approach shot is so accurate that it strikes the
edge of the cup, try to repair any damage to the surrounding
turf as much as possible. This repair may be done before anyone
putts, and does not incur any penalty. All repair work around the
cup should be done gently and judiciously. It should go without
saying that stomping on the ground around the hole as a means
of "repairing a ball mark" is not acceptable.

If you pull the flag out of the cup and the cup happens to

come up with the flag, simply push the cup back down. The top edge of the cup should be one inch below the surface of the green. If it's less than one inch below the surface, it's possible for a firm putt to hit the back of the cup and bounce out.

One other note: Sometimes the cup liner can come out of the hole when the pin is removed. If this happens while a putt is on its way to the hole and the ball drops into the unlined hole, the putt is good.

PINNING BLAME

Think handling the pin properly is a minor issue? Consider this story from one of our Post Golf Survey respondents. It proves that experience doesn't always equal good golf etiquette, and that even the low handicapper can sometimes use some polishing.

> **I was playing in a college golf tournament in Georgia, and was in a group with one of the nation's best golfers. From the first green all the way through the twelfth, this guy never replaced the flag in the hole. When he finished putting out, he would simply walk off the green and head to the next tee, without ever waiting for the rest of us. I finally confronted him about this on the thirteenth tee, and some words were exchanged. In the end, I realized that some of the best golfers can be guilty of some of the worst golf etiquette.**

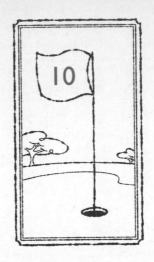

A TIME TO TALK AND A TIME TO KEEP QUIET

TALKING IS AN INTEGRAL PART OF THE GOLF EX-
PERIENCE. Walking the fairway, waiting between shots,
pausing at the turn, relaxing at the nineteenth hole—whether it's
a personal or business outing, these are perfect opportunities to
catch up on the latest news, enjoy the banter between friends, and
build relationships. As important as it is to be a good participant
in conversation, however, in golf, the key to being a successful
conversationalist begins with knowing when to be quiet.

DURING A SHOT

Whether you're on the tee, the fairway, or the green, as the players approach their balls, it's important for the incessant joke teller
or talker to take a break and save that priceless story or joke until
after everyone has taken their swings. This doesn't mean you can

start talking again as soon as the first golfer hits his shot. Wait until *all* the members of your group have made their shots before resuming your stroll down the fairway—and your story or joke.

My friend Doug is not what we would call a long-ball hitter. Even though he's a mild-mannered, relatively even-tempered fellow, I recently learned of something that I hadn't realized was frustrating him.

> **Conversation, chitchat, and stories are fine when everyone is walking up the fairway, but should not continue as the group approaches their second shots (or any shot, for that matter). As the short hitter, I routinely go first. All too often I find myself trying to concentrate on my shot while everyone is still chatting about whatever. What's really frustrating is that I have to hit with all the chatter still going on, and then the talk quiets down for everyone else's shot.**

THE JOKESTER

The jokester is oblivious of his effect on others. He's the guy who keeps telling an endless stream of stories and jokes—never just one. Slowly, the others start to realize that his jokes aren't for their amusement, but rather to keep the attention centered on him.

One survey respondent found that the jokester can even cost others strokes on their round.

> **My friend fancies himself a comedian, and he enjoys entertaining the entire foursome while**

we're playing golf. This includes cracking jokes right before you swing or even in the middle of your swing. Although we have many laughs together, it usually costs each player three to four strokes per side.

No matter how funny someone may be, there's such a thing as too much of a good thing.

THE PROBLEM WITH CELL PHONES

Unquestionably, people see cell phones as the single biggest cause of rudeness in today's world. A cell phone's ring alone intrudes on everyone nearby, breaking their concentration. When a person answers a call on a cell phone, he's ignoring the person he's with. When a person talks on a cell phone without excusing himself, he's disturbing those around him. With so much potential for rudeness, how you handle your cell phone has become one of today's most important etiquette issues—and this holds true on the golf course as much, if not more, than anywhere else. Here are a few reasons why you should consider leaving your cell phone at home or in the car the next time you stroll to the first tee.

Cell Phones Make You Lose Your Focus

First, think for a moment about how having your cell phone on during a round affects your own game. One day, I had a last-minute opportunity to be interviewed by a reporter from *USA Today*. That's an A-list interview that you can't pass up. However, I also had a tee time in forty-five minutes, so I gave the reporter the okay to call my cell phone, since my club has no policy banning cell phones on the course.

As we prepared to tee up our balls on the first hole, I explained my dilemma and my plan to our foursome: I had my phone set on vibrate. When the call came in, I would pick up my ball and step well away from the others, answer the phone, do the interview, and then rejoin them once the interview was finished.

They acquiesced, and we teed off. Even though everything had been arranged, I was still anxious, anticipating the phone ringing. My first shots weren't very good, and I quickly found myself heading for a triple bogey. Fortunately, the phone rang before I finished the first hole. I picked up my ball and did the interview, then rejoined the foursome on two. Even so, it took a couple of more holes before I was able to settle down and concentrate on my game.

I've learned through experience that focus in golf requires continuity. When continuity is interrupted, by a cell phone or anything else, focus is the first thing that's affected, and your game invariably suffers as a result.

Cell Phones Bother Other Players

The problem with using a cell phone out on the course is that everyone else sees it as rude, while the person using the phone believes he or she has a perfectly legitimate excuse that everyone else should understand. In reality, it doesn't work that way.

We were matched up with a single golfer one day. This gentleman is a local physician who is a fertility specialist. He took numerous calls while on the course, speaking loudly with his staff about patient information over the phone as we were playing.

The phenomenon of "cell-phone voice" adds to the problem. It's an observable fact that when people talk on a cell phone, their voice level skyrockets—and so does everyone else's annoyance.

Cell Phones Slow Down Play

A person talking on the cell phone isn't stepping up to her shot and playing when it's her turn. Thus the cell phone becomes a cause of slow play.

> **You are waiting to play your next hole, and you hear a loud voice yelling into his cell phone. The player doesn't appear to be interested in the game, but instead is slowing everyone else down.**

Cell Phones May Be Banned at the Facility Where You're Playing

I know of several facilities that have banned the use of cell phones anywhere at the club. Using one can actually jeopardize a member's good standing. If you're a visitor at any golfing establishment, always ask before leaving your cell phone on.

Bottom line: The cell phone causes far more trouble than it solves. Best advice: Turn it off and enjoy your game.

THE OTHER SIDE OF THE COIN

As easy as it is to rail against the use of cell phones, many people believe they do have a place on the golf course. Dr. Dave, one of the regulars in our foursome, is on call certain Thursday afternoons. We know this situation and respect it. If he couldn't have his phone with him, he couldn't play—an alternative that's unacceptable to us.

The key is really how he goes about it. If his phone does vibrate, he steps aside, takes the call, and then catches up with the rest of us. At no time does his cell-phone use bother our group or any other golfers on the course, thanks to the care he takes in moving to a place where he's alone and then speaking quietly. By being considerate and respectful, he makes it work for us all.

THE JURY IS STILL OUT—SO, IF YOU MUST . . .

Before you use a cell phone during a round of golf, first make sure that the course doesn't prohibit it. Second, if you must have your phone on, explain the situation to the rest of your group and then keep it on vibrate. Finally, be sure that when you use your phone, it in no way negatively affects any other golfers.

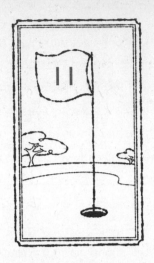

THE CHEAT AND THE SANDBAGGER

HONESTY IS ONE OF THE MOST IMPORTANT FACTORS IN DEVELOPING AND SUSTAINING RELATIONSHIPS THROUGHOUT LIFE. Do you want to associate with a person who is dishonest? Of course not. Good friendships and good business relationships are built on trust and truthfulness. The honest golfer—the golfer who respects and plays by the spirit of the game—is the golfer who's included in the weekly game and is invited to play in a member-guest tournament at another club. He's the one who builds friendships on the course that become lifelong friendships off the course, and the one who discovers business coming his way because of his conduct on the course.

PRIDE IN FOLLOWING THE RULES?

It seems as if there is a "catch me if you can" philosophy that can be found in almost every sport. Imagine a hockey player banning himself to the sin bin for throwing an elbow or tripping an opponent, or a basketball player handing the ball to an opponent because he double-dribbled but wasn't whistled by a referee.

Not very likely. Golfers, however, take pride in the game for the very fact that it *doesn't* have referees or judges. Our Post Golf Survey respondents spoke eloquently of their pride in playing a game that honors honesty and sportsmanship.

> **The best part of playing this wonderful game of golf is that it is a "gentleman's" game. Women and men know the rules and call themselves on rules violations. No other sport can claim this most honest of approaches to a sport. Because of this, there's a tremendous amount of integrity among those who play this great game.**

> **Calling yourself for a dubbed shot in the trees, or hearing your partner or opponent report that they had an extra shot you may not have seen, warms the heart and supports this great self-ruling game.**

Integrity is a word you rarely see applied to a sport. But in golf, integrity is everything. When you play with integrity— when you respect the rules and play by them, when you call an infraction on yourself, when you report your score accurately rather than shaving a few strokes off your round—you gain the respect of your playing partners and, just as important, you can take pride in yourself. In golf, these feelings of respect and pride matter. They're what make the game great.

RULING THE RULES

Every golfer should take time to read the USGA's *The Rules of Golf.* Better yet, read the decisions based on the rules, as well. You can buy books on the subject, or go to the USGA Web site (www.usga.com) to find all the rules and related decisions.

Doing this will make you a better golfer: Not only will you be sure of what to do in various circumstances, but you'll also know how to respond if a competitor challenges you, or if you find yourself in a situation where you're not sure of your options.

THE CHEAT

While golf is a gentleman's game in which golfers are expected to call penalties against themselves, it's also true that there are those nefarious individuals who cheat—and their actions definitely frustrate their fellow golfers. Dropped balls, strokes taken but not counted, improved lies—these are all part of the cheater's arsenal, and they all chip away at the integrity of the game every time they're employed. (See "When Is a Rule Bender a Cheat?" page 189.)

Calling a Friend a Cheater

Most of the time, golfers know when someone is cheating—and yet often they say nothing about it. The conflicting emotions involved are understandable: You don't want to be the victim of cheating, but you also don't want to hurt a friendship. Besides, calling out the cheat will inevitably lead to a nasty confrontation, and who really wants to deal with that?

IT'S NOT JUST ABOUT CHEATING TO WIN

Bob had been invited to play with Jerry in a member-guest tournament at Jerry's club. Unfortunately, they weren't doing well. At the seventeenth hole, Jerry's tee shot rolled into a fresh, deep divot. Bob watched in horror as Jerry took one look at his ball and rolled it out of the divot. He hoped nobody had seen Jerry's indiscretion.

"Jerry," he called out, "what are you doing? You can't do that. We're playing in a tournament. Put it back, please." Jerry looked over at Bob and shook his head. "No way," he replied. "I may be out of contention, but I'm sure as heck not going to have us finish last."

Whether you're gunning for first place or trying to avoid last place, cheating is cheating. In one instant, Jerry has jeopardized his friendship with Bob, he has risked the team's being disqualified, and he has turned a fun event with his friend into a stress-filled, unpleasant experience. Bad choice, Jerry.

We have a member at our club who always moves his ball to achieve a better lie. I personally witnessed him roll his ball with his foot until it was out of a low spot. He's also infamous for picking up his ball on the green before he marks it and then marking it several inches closer to the hole. But no one has the courage to call him out.

Often, in a tricky situation like this, it's not a matter of whether you say something, but how: "Jim, I can't believe you'd claim a five there! You had at least seven strokes—what kind of cheat are you?" might be a little too direct. Here's a softer alternative that still addresses the problem: "Jim, a five? You had a drive. Your second shot was in the water. Three out. Four onto the green and then a three putt. I think that's seven." Stick to the facts. Don't assume the worst of the person and attack him personally.

During a friendly game, if you encounter the ball dropper or the lie improver, you should address the issue at the moment it happens: "Jim, what's going on? I saw that ball drop out of your hand. Do me and yourself a favor and pick it up, please." Or before he hits the improved lie: "Jim, what a shame your tee ball ended up in that divot. Too bad we're not playing lift, clean, and place. You really should be playing that ball from where it lay." Express yourself calmly, without anger. Your focus should be on stopping the cheating and then moving on.

How to Lose Friends Forever

I'm not sure if cheaters realize they're risking much more than being caught in the act of cheating. Their actions are certainly jeopardizing their long-term relationships with their friends— and their reputation will precede them with other golfers in the club, as well.

Cheating to win in golf is absolutely unacceptable. On two occasions, I've terminated friendships with people whom I've known for years because of their

golfing dishonesty. Fortunately, the reality is that the great majority of golfers are honorable.

Dropping Balls

I must say, I've never witnessed a golfer intentionally drop a ball while searching for a lost ball and then declare it to be the ball he was looking for. But plenty of golfers have. When you see someone doing this, it's important to call him on it right there on the spot. In friendly play, you can opt to allow the perpetrator to pick up the dropped ball and then either play a lost ball or continue searching for the ball. In a tournament, you should advise the perpetrator that you witnessed the action and are reporting him to a tournament official or the tournament committee. By not reporting him, you're being complicit in his action. Imagine if you saw someone cheat but said nothing, and he then went on to win the club championship. That should not be allowed to happen. (See "For the Integrity of the Field: When It Doesn't Pay to Be the Nice Guy," page 154.)

JUST AMAZING

I once played with an idiot who thought that when you gave him a short putt he didn't have to count the putt as a stroke.

The Stroke Shaver

Here's the person I don't understand.

"What did you have on that hole, Henry?" I'll ask.

"I think a five" is the answer that comes back at me. Hmmmm?

"Henry, didn't you have a six? Your first ball was out of bounds, and you reloaded."

"Whatever," says Henry.

Whatever? It matters. Keeping an accurate score of your shots and reporting the right number of shots is an integral part of the game. The great Roberto De Vicenzo lost the opportunity to be in a play-off for the 1968 Masters title because of a scoring error. After De Vicenzo's card was signed and turned in, the official scorers discovered that his score for the seventeenth hole was recorded as a 4 when it should have been a 3. The higher score prevailed, and he missed a play-off by one stroke. While his mistake has become legendary, De Vicenzo also made one of the best-known responses in the history of the game upon learning of the error (which was initially made by his opponent, not himself): "Oh. What a stupid I am!" He didn't blame the marker for writing down the wrong score; instead, he blamed himself for not catching the error before signing the card. This extraordinary display of tact and sportsmanship has become a part of golf lore forever.

Sadly, not everyone is as intent as De Vicenzo was on upholding the spirit of the game. Post Golf Survey respondents told story after story of competitors in tournaments, opponents in friendly matches, and friends during a fun round who, unlike De Vicenzo, intentionally claimed the wrong lower score on a hole.

Everyone hates a cheater. I have witnessed someone celebrating his best round, knowing full well that he shaved at least five strokes off his score—not to mention the generous gimme putts along the way.

When playing in a golf tournament in college, my
opponent cheated when I asked what he had on
a hole. It frustrated me, since I felt like I had to
constantly watch him after that because I knew I
couldn't trust him.

When playing a nine-hole match during a ladies'
league, a competitor gave an incorrect score.
When I asked her to review her score, she did not
remember a poor chip that resulted in the need
for another chip. She conceded that she may have
miscounted a shot, but certainly seemed unsure of
my count. The rest of the match was very awkward
and not enjoyable.

What Goes Around Comes Around

Sometimes the course metes out justice all by itself.

This was told to me by a friend who was caddying.
On a hole that had a sharp dogleg to the right,
a player for whom he was carrying a bag hit his
second shot over the trees, cutting the corner to
the green. The player assumed the ball had landed
in the woods and went to search for it. He "found"
it and played it to the green. When my friend, the
caddie, got to the pin to remove it, the player's
original ball was in the hole. The caddie quietly
removed the ball and returned it to the player.
Because he'd cheated, he couldn't take credit for

**the eagle that he got by holing the ball on a blind
second shot.**

This person was fortunate the caddie found his ball and was
discreet about returning it to him. In a regular foursome, the cat
would have been out of the bag, and at the very least the offender
would have been the recipient of a significant amount of trash
talk.

THE SANDBAGGER

Next to the cheat, no one is more annoying than the sandbagger
—the golfer who always adds a few strokes to his score so his
handicap is higher than it ought to be. There are two reasons why
a golfer may do this:

- To gain an advantage in a tournament by being
  placed in a higher flight, where he's more likely to
  win

- To be given additional strokes in a net tournament
  (see Chapter 15, "In a Tournament: When
  Everything *Really* Counts," pages 148–156)

It seems as if every course has a few sandbaggers. In tournament play, handicap committees try to ferret them out. Pro shops
will make every effort to be sure handicaps for the tournament
are up-to-date and accurate, and tournament committees can
adjust handicaps if they feel it's necessary.

But what about a golfer who sandbags in the friendly
Saturday game? My experience is that, in these cases, it's the
sandbagger who ultimately suffers. The other golfers sometimes

choose not to play with the sandbagger. Or they may refuse to engage in a friendly wager. Or they hoot and howl on the first tee and demand a handicap adjustment before play begins. When three buddies are all saying, "Seventeen? Give me a break! Mid-eighties or better the past few weeks is *not* a seventeen," suddenly the 17 becomes a 14 and equilibrium is restored.

On the other side of the coin, one thing that I find especially frustrating is when I have a good round going, and I sink a putt for my third par in a row, and suddenly I hear, "That's some seventeen," from an opponent who wants to knock me off my game. The opponent I appreciate is the one who can compliment me on the good game I'm having without implying that I've fudged my handicap. Better yet, don't say anything—because it might jinx the great round I have going.

THE FAUX SANDBAGGER

 The faux sandbagger is the opposite of the sandbagger. The faux sandbagger carries a handicap that is *lower* than it should be. High-scoring rounds become practice rounds and conveniently aren't posted. The end result is a lower handicap than is warranted.

This person hurts two people: himself, and anyone who is his partner in a tournament or in a friendly Saturday game.

The best practice: Post your scores—all your scores—and let the chips fall where they may.

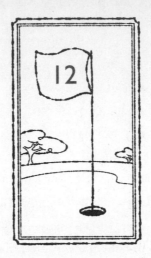

"SON, YOU'RE NOT GOOD ENOUGH TO THROW CLUBS"

IF GOLF IS SUCH A GENTLEMAN'S GAME, WHY IS IT THAT SO MANY GOLFERS, MYSELF INCLUDED, TREAD ON THE DARK SIDE AND LET TEMPER TAKE OVER AS A RESULT OF POOR PLAY? When this happens, we do irrational things—often to our clubs, but sometimes to the course, to the carts, or, even worse, to other golfers or ourselves.

I know that whenever I get carried away with my emotions, I feel foolish afterward for my display, and end up either trying to make light of it or apologizing. I wish I'd had a wise old golfer to counsel me when I was young and learning the game, the way this Post Golf Survey respondent did.

I once threw a club out of frustration. I was playing with a wise old golfer who put his arm around my shoulders and whispered, "Son, you're not good enough to throw clubs."

THE ANTIDOTE FOR TEMPER TANTRUMS

You can combat temper tantrums with a little rational thought, an attitude shift, and a deep breath.

Rational thought. If you think first instead of simply acting without thinking, you're more likely to avoid losing your temper.

An attitude shift. It's just a game—so treat it that way. If your round is going south in a hurry, try taking a few minutes to appreciate your good fortune at being out on a beautiful golf course enjoying the company of your friends. (For more on this, see Chapter 1, "We're All in This Together," pages 1–11.)

A deep breath. When you feel yourself starting to lose it, do whatever you need to do to get control of yourself before you act. Some people learn to count to ten. Others take deep, measured breaths—breathing in through the nose, out through the mouth—to slow the heart rate and calm the soul. You might as well give it a try on the course. After all, a calm, relaxed body is sure to play better than a tight, stressed body.

TOP FIVE REASONS NOT TO LOSE YOUR TEMPER

At the very least, a display of temper can result in a higher score or lost equipment. More seriously, it can lead to the loss of friendships, isolation from other golfers, or injury. Your goal should always be to avoid losing your temper while playing. Here are five reasons to stay cool.

1. You'll Catch More Flies with Honey Than with Vinegar

Who wants to play with an angry, stressed-out golfer? No one. During those rounds where someone loses it, I've noticed that, first, he tends to get left alone on the course, and second, if it's repetitive behavior, he tends to get left off the invitation list.

> A stranger joined our group to play and was very rude. He cursed after every poor shot—which happened a lot—and took forever to look for balls that were impossible to find. He just had a terrible attitude. We ended up politely excusing ourselves and playing ahead of him, leaving him to play by himself.

2. Your Temper Tantrum Can Damage the Course

You'll see them everywhere: the marks of an angry golfer. Tee boxes have gouges in them where a golfer has slammed his club in disgust after yet another horrid drive. The same goes for fairways. Tree bark has been mashed into a pulp with the sole of an iron; traps have large splash marks caused by a sand wedge after a flubbed shot.

One survey respondent even witnessed a disgruntled player take his anger out on a green with old metal spikes (soft spikes can do just as much damage).

> I once saw a golfer drag his metal spikes across several yards of green because he missed a putt. The damage was as horrendous as his behavior.

Damage to the course makes play for those following more difficult if their ball lands in your gouge, more unpleasant because they have to view the results of the tantrum thrower's anger, and more expensive, since ultimately, it adds to the maintenance costs for the course for which all the golfers pay.

3. Your Temper Tantrum Affects the Other Players

Maybe it's time for golfers to stand up for themselves. It's painful to hear how thoroughly the game can be spoiled by people who are unable to control their emotions.

> I play golf with my husband quite often. Most of the time, we end up playing with a twosome of men who we don't know. The round will typically start nice and politely; but as it progresses and balls get lost, terrible shots fall into the rough, and putts get missed, the men we're playing with seem to lose their manners. I'm then stuck with two

strangers who are swearing and often flying off the
handle, and a husband who's trying his best to keep
things neutral. What should I do or say when this
happens? It's not only distressing to hear, but it also
affects my golf.

It is inexcusable for these louts to ruin this woman's game
or anyone else's. Golfers being affected by other golfers who lose
control should say in an assertive voice: "I'm sorry, but we aren't
here to listen to that kind of language and to put up with your ill
temper. Please, stop or drop back and play on your own, so we
can enjoy our game."

4. Your Temper Tantrum Could Foul Up Your Prospects

When you think of building relationships on the golf course,
you think in terms of business, not social opportunities like a
first date—but it happens. Either way, people take the measure
of each other according to how they conduct themselves on the
course. The next time you're tempted to let a few choice words fly
after making a lousy shot, imagine how this would be received if
you were on a blind date on the golf course.

While I was in grad school, a fellow student
thought her brother and I would be the perfect
pair, so she arranged a golf "date" for us. He was a
nice-looking, well-mannered guy, until he hit a shot
he really didn't like—at which point he threw his
club, swore, and was unpleasant for the rest of the
day. Needless to say, we didn't "date" again. Since

then, I've often witnessed players (usually men,
including even tournament professionals) pounding
clubs into the ground or throwing their clubs. It
just seems immature.

 Business Golf Tip

Win by Controlling Your Temper

When you're playing with your regular group, when the going gets
tough, they may cut you a break when you lose your temper. But
think for a minute about how your loss of control appears to the
client, prospect, or boss you're playing with. Is your foul temper
an example of how you will run that team, or work with that client?
Bottom line: Curb your temper and save the deal, contract, or
promotion.

5. Your Temper Tantrum Is Dangerous to You and Your Fellow Golfers

It almost goes without saying, but I'll say it anyway: Temper
tantrums on the golf course can lead to serious injury for the tantrum thrower and for others who are nearby. What happened in
the following story is bad enough—but imagine what could have
occurred if the shaft had hit another golfer instead. The thought
alone is reason enough not to hit a tree, or slam a club on the
ground, or throw a club in anger ever again.

In a betting match, a player became so incensed
after a bad shot that he threw his club at a bench.
The club snapped in two and the shaft impaled
him in the leg, causing a severe puncture wound.

HUMOR: THE ANTIDOTE TO TEMPER

Humor can go a long way toward improving your overall outlook on a round of golf, good or bad. Doug's favorite approach is to inflict a little self-deprecating humor on himself, thus keeping it light for the rest of us. The par-4 sixteenth on our home course has two fairway bunkers, one to the left about 110 yards out, and one to the right about 190 yards out. Doug routinely drives one of two places. The first and most usual place is 10 yards to the left and just short of the right bunker. He jokes that he keeps a park bench there along with a beer cooler to quench his thirst, after hitting within 3 feet of this spot forty to fifty times a year. Sometimes, however, he spices up the hole by hitting into the left bunker. Being barely 110 yards from the tee, it's rare that anyone else ever hits it there, but somehow his ball manages to find it.

Doug explains how he handles what could easily be a temper tantrum moment as follows: "I get a kick out of the comments and fun poked at my incredibly short and commercial drive to the right, or my horrible drive to the left. I always get through the gales of laughter by letting everyone know that I *own* that left-hand bunker. No one else comes near it. Then I'll challenge them—and pick myself up at the same time—by declaring that I can still usually par in from there and win the hole. No one believes me . . . or do they?"

Doug adds that this humorous banter takes all the frustration and anger out of his poor drive. "Anger on the course—no other players want to hear it, be near it, or have to play their own game through it!" he says flatly. "Get a grip and let the *whole* foursome enjoy their day on the course, even if you're struggling. In tournaments, I usually remember this, and act more responsibly toward the others as a result. No one needs to endure a spoiled crybaby while they're playing."

GOLF COURSE JUSTICE

One of my most embarrassing moments on a golf course occurred when I took out my frustrations over my putting on my putter. No, I didn't wrap it around a tree (although in retrospect I wish I had, because then I could have put a new shaft on it and still had the putter). Instead, I was foolish enough, after having missed yet another easy putt, to walk off the green and hit the ground angrily with the putter.

Normally, this action would "merely" have been bad behavior on my part. Several years earlier, however, I'd been practicing putting in our pro shop with a variety of putters. Suddenly, there in the rack, I noticed a putter I'd never seen before. A brand-new model made by Odyssey, it was a beautiful black putter with a mallet-style head. I tried it a few times and bought it on the spot.

Now, it so happens that when this Odyssey putter first came out, the entire head was made of the black material that's now only used as an insert. Very shortly thereafter, Odyssey stopped making the putter with the all-black head and instead started making the putters we all know so well, with an insert at the impact point on the putter face.

As I swung that putter down in frustration, I wasn't thinking about the rare piece of golf equipment I owned; I was simply mad as hell. The head hit the ground with a satisfying thump, and then split apart into a couple of pieces where the shaft went into the head.

Not very many people in the golf world are lucky enough

to own one of the solid-black Odyssey putters. Today, there's one less of them. I don't slam clubs into the ground anymore.

From Bad to Worse

Does the golf course have a mind and soul of its own (see Chapter 4, "Respect the Course," pages 36–46)? It seems as though it just might, given the number of times the course gets the better of golfers who abuse it. Here's a brief tale of how a disrespected tree did one golfer in.

> The following is an absolutely true story. A good friend missed a short putt and, in a show of disgust, tossed his putter up into a tree. He then took his driver and tossed it at the putter in hopes of knocking the putter out of the tree. Amazingly, his driver got stuck in the tree, too. He then took off his left shoe and threw it at the putter, and the left shoe got stuck in said tree. He then took off his right shoe and threw it at the putter and the same thing happened. He turned around to find that a golf course maintenance worker was laughing uncontrollably at him!

The course doesn't always take away, however. Sometimes it gives back, too, if a golfer has the right karma. Jay makes his own clubs and, rightfully, takes great pride in his skill. It was raining on the fateful day in question, but Jay is an avid golfer, so he was out there. The grips on his clubs had gotten progressively wetter and wetter. He got up to the tee on one hole and took out

his newly made driver, swung hard, heard a solid click, and then realized he no longer had a club in his hands. He watched incredulously as his new driver sailed out over a pond adjacent to the tee. Like a javelin sticking into the ground, the handle penetrated the surface of the water and imbedded itself in the muck, with the head of the driver wagging back and forth just above the surface.

He was already wet, so Jay marched out into the pond (which was waist deep when he got to the driver), retrieved his club, and finished his round. The course could easily have swallowed that club whole, but instead it showed mercy and gave Jay back his driver.

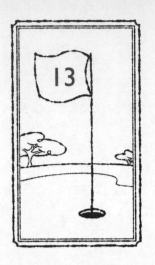

TO COACH OR NOT TO COACH?

IS IT BETTER TO SAY SOMETHING TO A FELLOW GOLFER WHEN YOU SEE HER DOING SOMETHING YOU BELIEVE IS HURTING HER GAME—OR SHOULD YOU KEEP YOUR MOUTH SHUT?

That's the question, in a nutshell.

A suggestion on golf mechanics can be invaluable, but when and how the advice is offered will make a huge difference in how it's received. My putting is a perfect example of how, on two occasions, a little coaching from golfers who I know well really helped my game.

COACHING ON THE COURSE

Offering advice on the course is dicey at best during a friendly game of golf. But during a tournament, be very careful to whom you offer advice, such as what club to play or or how to hit a shot. Other than to a partner, it is against the rules to give advice. Information, such as if an opponent is teeing his ball up in front of the tee markers, is acceptable.

I used to be a good putter. Then, as happens to many of us, about three years ago I suddenly found myself three- and four-putting regularly. Doug is one of the best putters I know. He took it upon himself to work with me on the practice green and on the course. The way he coached me on the course was perfect. He didn't critique every putt I made. In fact, he often didn't say anything at all. When he did say something, it was always done quietly when others weren't nearby. These gentle reminders helped me focus on what I needed to do without embarrassing me. After all, I already knew I'd missed yet another putt. I certainly didn't need him to make a public event about the correction he was suggesting—something he understood implicitly.

While my putting improved, I was still prone to "yipping" the ball, jerking my hands at the last minute and throwing my putt off. I tried gripping the putter with my right hand low and with my right hand high, but nothing worked. One day, my brother began extolling the virtues of the claw grip. I nodded my head and kept right on putting the way I always had, but he still managed to mention his dedication to the claw grip once or twice on each round. After several rounds of listening repeatedly to his comments, I decided to give the grip a try. For a right-handed golfer, the left hand is in the same position. However, the fingers of the right hand are placed on top of the shaft instead of underneath it. This placement of the fingers keeps the golfer from opening or closing the face of the club as he putts.

At this point, I digress to give you the only piece of mechanical golf-swing advice you'll encounter in this book: If you yip, if you miss putts you know you should make, or if you approach each putt with trepidation, do yourself a favor and go to your practice putting green and try the claw grip. It is, in a word, magic. The claw grip prevents a golfer from twisting the putter head at impact and causing the putt to go off-line.

There's one thing I promise if you play golf with me: I won't give you any advice, not even about putting. Unless you ask about the claw grip—in which case, you've given me permission to tell you about it.

WHO NOT TO COACH

Coaching another golfer is a tricky thing at best. It may be possible to give advice to someone you know well, but even then you've got to be careful (see "When to Coach?" page 135). People *not* to coach include:

- That slight acquaintance or stranger who is joining you for a round that day
- Your children
- Your spouse
- Any member of the opposite sex

WHEN TO COACH?

If you're going to do it, be very conscious of *how* and *when* and *to whom* you do it. On the course, immediately after I've made a horrible swing, the last thing I want to hear, even from one of my playing companions, is: "You know, Peter, you're really wrapping that club way past parallel. You ought to try to shorten your backswing." Do you really think I couldn't see my clubhead with my left eye as it wrapped way around me?

A much better time to give advice is during a quiet moment, such as when you're walking between holes, or after a round is done, when the competitive fires have died down and cool reason can prevail. Here's how one survey respondent described the ideal approach.

> I was casting my club and hitting everything off the heel, shanking the ball all over the course, when a guy talked to me about hitting down on the ball and making my divot halfway up the ball. His advice changed the way I play. The greatest thing was that he showed me this on the range after the round. He told me that no one wants to get constant coaching on the course. He made sure he gave me pointers at a time I was more likely to accept the teaching.

 Business Golf Tip

Keep Your Mouth Shut

When you're in a business golf setting, curb your enthusiasm to offer advice unless someone specifically asks for your input—

especially if you are a better player than those around you. Instead, let your game speak for itself. After all, if you give unwanted advice on the course, perhaps you'll treat clients and prospects tactlessly, as well. That's not the image you want your boss to have of you.

If, on the other hand, your boss makes the mistake of offering you advice on *your* game, the better part of valor is to bite your tongue, smile, and politely say, "Thank you."

Don't offer advice on the course unless you're sure it's wanted, and even then offer it only to someone you know well (see "Who Not to Coach," page 134). The only way to be sure it's okay to offer advice is to wait for the golfer to say something that indicates he's open to a suggestion, and then ask politely if he really wants one.

Once in a while, for example, I'll notice a certain playing partner starting to pick his club up steeply at the start of a drive instead of sweeping it back. The result is usually a lousy shot, a few expletives, and a healthy dose of frustration. The last time I saw this, I waited until we started walking down the fairway and his frustration had eased a bit. That's the first key to offering advice: Do it privately. He opened the opportunity for me to say something by grousing, "I've fallen apart. I don't know what's going wrong." That's the second key to offering advice: Wait for the person to ask for it. At that point, I quietly said: "I think I noticed something. Do you want to hear it?" That's the third key to offering advice: Make sure they want advice before you offer it. A grumbled "sure" gave me my opening. His next drive featured a smooth takeaway and a much better result. I smiled and didn't say another word. That's the fourth key: Don't keep repeating the advice—once is enough.

TWO EAGLES FOR YOUR THOUGHTS

One survey respondent described how he successfully offered a little help by asking first. In this case, the result was truly amazing.

> I was playing with an average woman golfer who had a hard time making pars. On one par-5 hole, I suggested I assist her with each shot by helping her with her alignment, and she agreed. In the process, my own third shot went into the cup for an eagle. The players on the green had waved me on [see "Strategies for Speeding Up Play," page 75], and when the ball went in, they went wild. Once the excitement died down, I walked over to my companion and helped line up her third shot. (In case you're wondering, my second shot was lousy, so I wasn't any farther down the fairway than she was after our second shots.) Lo and behold, she nailed it right onto the green and into the cup. Now the golfers on the green went absolutely ballistic. I've never seen two eagles made on a single hole, one on top of the other, ever—and I've played golf for over fifty-five years. Needless to say, the woman has never forgotten that moment, either.

A PIECE OF ADVICE ABOUT ADVICE FROM DOUG

"Maybe you should add more of a warning to this chapter," Doug told me after reading it over. So here's his warning: "Giving advice of any sort is more likely to get a bad reaction than good, and is probably flawed instruction anyway. Here's the thing: Recreational golf is not meant to be a coaching platform, and your advice is likely to be wrong for that person. People go to their local pros for advice because that way they get to pick the instructor's personality and gender and choose the time when it's right for them to get some coaching. Furthermore, the course is the worst place to work on your swing. Do this on the range. When you're playing a round, just try to score as well as you can during the game. That's where the real enjoyment is—a low score still can be achieved with a big slice or swinging the stick at twenty miles per hour. Finally, how can your advice be valid when your own swing is a disaster? Would you like the guy to turn around and start telling you about your flaws on the next tee?"

DON'T BEAT THE LOVE OF THE GAME OUT OF YOUR CHILD

Coaching friends is tough enough. But for some reason, coaching spouses and children seems to bring out the worst in golfers. One Post Golf Survey respondent was particularly frustrated at, in his words, "watching a father scream at his ten-year-old child for not lining up his putt properly." What's the point of behavior like this? Nothing good comes from berating a child—or anyone else, for that matter. The child loses respect for the parent, while other golfers who see the episode are aghast. What's more, the child may well end up resenting not only the parent but the game of golf as well.

Another respondent writes:

> I was playing with a father and his son in Hilton Head. The young man's older brother was captain of his high school golf team and had earned a place on his college team. This poor teen could barely concentrate because his father was constantly correcting and berating him. It was the kind of thing that shouldn't have been done in private, let alone in front of a perfect stranger. I felt sorry for this young man, and I wondered how long it would be before his father verbally beat his love of the game out of him.

RISKY BUSINESS

If the person you want to coach is your significant other, the danger just multiplied tenfold. I've rarely witnessed a person give advice to their significant other and have it be well received. Simply put, the love of your life may not love you quite so much if you try to teach him or her how to play golf. On the other side of the coin, I've seen steam come out of the ears of many a person when unsolicited advice was offered by their life partner.

My advice: Leave the task of instructing your spouse or partner to a neutral third party—your local golf pro.

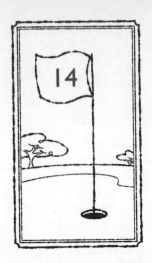

AT A TOURNAMENT: THE GOOD SPECTATOR

ATTENDING A PROFESSIONAL GOLF TOURNAMENT IS A GREAT WAY TO EXPERIENCE GOLF AND ENJOY BEING AT A BEAUTIFUL VENUE. How lucky the fans are who attend the Masters every April and get to witness the Georgia spring in full bloom. They also get to see the best of the best in the golfing world compete on one of the most challenging courses anywhere.

As with any sport, the majority of spectators at golf tournaments abide by the rules and are respectful of the players. And as with any sport, there are also those few louts who make watching the tournament unpleasant and participating difficult because their antics distract the players from concentrating on the game at hand. It's not hard to be a good spectator at a golf tournament: Just show the same consideration for the players and the event that golfers show each other.

BEFORE YOU ARRIVE

When you bring anywhere from 20,000 to 40,000 spectators into a venue to watch a bunch of golfers play eighteen holes, you need a few basic rules to govern conduct—rules that will allow everyone to enjoy the event and give the players the optimum opportunity to perform. Those rules start affecting you before you even arrive at the course. For this reason, you should plan on leaving a few things at home or in your car that you might ordinarily consider bringing to other sporting events.

A camera. You cannot bring a camera onto the grounds during any day of the actual tournament—which is Thursday through Sunday for a PGA Tour event. Cameras are permitted during practice rounds.

A backpack. In this post-9/11 age, the time and effort it would take to search thousands of backpacks would make getting the people through the gates impossible.

Cell phones and other electronic communication devices. A player can hear the sound of a phone ringing from several hundred yards away. One is bad enough. Imagine the distraction if dozens were ringing as Tiger or Phil started addressing his shot. Imagine the cacophony of the ringing, the volume of people's phone voices, and the inane conversations that all the other spectators would be subjected to.

If you don't leave these objects at home, you will create delays at the entrance gates as the security people find them and then have to argue with you over the fact that they can't let you in. You'll annoy the spectators who are held up getting inside as the result of your mistake, and you'll begin your day in a stressed mood. Even if you do manage to sneak a camera or cell phone past security, if you get caught with it once you're inside, you may be ejected. It's just not worth the hassle.

FIVE GUIDELINES FOR WATCHING A GOLF TOURNAMENT

1. *Don't ask for autographs.* It's okay to seek autographs before the players reach the practice area and after they've signed their scorecard and left the scorer's area, but never in between. Often there's an area set aside for autograph signing. If so, go there.

2. *Don't try to speak to the players.* The proximity spectators have to players—another great thing about attending a golf tournament—can make it seem as if exchanging a few words would be okay. It's not. While it's acceptable to offer encouragement to the players such as "Keep it up, Phil!" or "Great birdie, Tiger!" avoid trying to engage them directly with comments like "Hey, Tiger, what club did you hit?" or "Hey, Vijay, my son goes to the same school as yours."

3. *Don't offer advice to the players.* This is a special subcategory of the previous guideline. The player knows better than you do—much, much better— exactly how to play a shot to fit his game. Your suggestion is obnoxiously superfluous, to say the least.

4. *Don't touch a player's ball, ever.* Players' shots don't always land "inside the ropes." Watch the ball, stay out of its way as it lands, and don't think you're being a help by moving it, kicking it, catching it, or stopping it.

5. *Stand still when the players are hitting shots.* Something as seemingly innocuous as your shifting position for a better view can catch a player's attention at just the wrong moment. Players will tell you that one of the most annoying things spectators do at tournaments is laugh, talk, and move about when they're trying to hit. Whenever a player is addressing the ball, stand still and be quiet.

A BALL IN YOUR LAP

Occasionally, you'll see a ball literally land on a spectator. If that happens to you, don't move, even if the ball is sitting in your lap. Instead, wait for the player to arrive. He'll mark the spot on the ground directly below where the ball is in your lap. Then, when you do get up, he can drop the ball in that place.

IN ADDITION . . .

Spectators should also keep an eye out for the following transgressions.

Watch your language. Children do attend golf events. And in the crowded confines of a large gallery, adults who might be offended by foul language won't necessarily be able to "move away."

Don't make negative comments about the players. It's likely that among the spectators following any given golfer will be members of his family and some of his friends. Be considerate of what impact your words might have on them before you let fly with a disparaging comment.

Cheer, don't jeer. Golf has a great tradition of complimenting golfers' shots, and, as a rule, crowds at tournaments cheer loudly in appreciation of players' efforts. Recently, though, there have been sporadic instances of jeering from the gallery—especially at international events such as the Ryder Cup or Presidents Cup matches. Unfortunately, it's showing its ugly face at some of the regular tour events as well. Jeering has no place in the game. Perpetrators can, should be, and have been removed for such behavior.

Dress appropriately. Wear golf attire at a golf venue. (See Chapter 3, " 'You're Out!' and Other Intricacies of Golf Attire," pages 25–35.)

Don't over-imbibe. It appears as if the combination of spectating and alcohol is here to stay, since beer and liquor sales are now such an important revenue stream for professional sports. Even though alcohol is served at a sports event, however, doesn't mean that drunken behavior should be or is tolerated. At golf tournaments, inebriated spectators will be asked to leave.

Be careful where you smoke. I'm sure no player appreciates a puff of smoke wafting across him as he addresses his ball. And even though they're outdoors, some of your fellow spectators may also be very disturbed by your smoke. If you have to have a cigarette, move away from the gallery and be aware of the wind direction.

Watch your shadow. If it's late afternoon, your shadow may be in a player's line of sight or actually on him or his ball. If you can't move, it becomes more important than ever to stay perfectly still.

Don't block other people's views. Often the gallery at a pro tournament can be large and deep. Take care to give the people behind you a chance to see. Be especially careful if you're carrying a shade or rain umbrella. There's nothing more infuriating than the person with a large umbrella who blocks the view of people all around him.

Don't touch that chair. At the Masters, there's a tradition that says a folding chair holds a place for the owner when the owner isn't there. Other spectators shouldn't move that chair. This tradition is now extending to other tournaments, as well. It makes sense: The person sitting in that chair may be in that position for several hours watching all the golfers go by, and it stands to reason that he'll need a brief bathroom break or a chance to get something to eat from time to time.

THE FUTURE OF GOLF SPECTATING?

The sixteenth hole at the FBR Open holds a special place in golf spectating. The tournament is held at the TPC Scottsdale

Stadium Course in Arizona, and the sixteenth is a par 3. What makes it special is the insanely large and raucous crowd that surrounds the hole. Some players play to the crowd here, egging them on. Others are intimidated by the throng. One thing is for sure, though: The sixteenth is unique in golf. While the crowd does quiet down for the tee shot itself, pandemonium seems to break out immediately afterward—especially with a great shot or a very wayward shot.

Compare this crowd's behavior to that of the gallery surrounding the twelfth hole at the Masters. One is loud and judgmental, the other reserved and appreciative. The behavior at the sixteenth has become legendary and isn't likely to stop, but it also should not represent the future of golf spectating.

AT A LOCAL TOURNAMENT

The same guidelines that dictate your behavior at a professional tournament apply when you watch fellow golfers compete on your local course. The most noticeable difference will be the lack of crowds. There may be only a smattering of people following the final group on the final day. Yet these players deserve the same opportunity as the top professionals to concentrate on their game.

Don't try to speak to the players. They need to concentrate, so leave them alone and enjoy watching them play. There'll be plenty of time for talking after the round is finished.

Don't offer advice to the players. They're already aware of any advice you might think to give them. The distraction you'll cause will be far more problematic than any conceivable benefit from the advice.

Don't touch a player's ball, ever. It's no more appropriate to improve a lie or stop a ball from rolling out of bounds in a local tournament than it is in a PGA Tour event. The player (or, in certain circumstances, his caddie) is the only person who should touch his ball while it's in play. Ever.

Stand still when the players are hitting shots. You're close to the action, so even the slightest movement during a backswing could distract the player.

Shut off cell phones and be careful with cameras. Don't even have your phone on vibrate—the noise can still be heard. And don't take pictures while a player is swinging.

IT'S NOT AGAINST THE RULES . . .

But maybe it ought to be. The people running tournaments seem to have found a way to get the spectators waving signs containing biblical verse out of range of the television cameras. So why can't they shut up the idiots who yell, "You da man!" or "Get in the hole!" after virtually every shot?

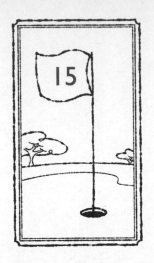

IN A TOURNAMENT: WHEN EVERYTHING *REALLY* COUNTS

DOES ANYTHING CHANGE WHEN YOU FIND YOUR-SELF PLAYING IN A TOURNAMENT? Do you play differently with your regular foursome than you do in an organized event?

The answer to both questions is a resounding "Yes." Playing a little loose with the rules, yukking it up with your friends, taking a mulligan or a gimme here and there—these behaviors are all a natural part of "friendly" golf, but they are *not* acceptable when "the game is on." Being aware of the following key points will make your tournament experience a fun and positive one, and will also give you the best chance of doing well—and perhaps even winning.

KNOW THE RULES OF GOLF

While the rules of golf matter any time, knowing them in a tournament can mean the difference between successfully navigating a situation and being disqualified. Remember, if you have a disagreement with an opponent about a situation, always keep the focus on the facts of the situation. Don't let it become a heated argument.

The rules govern the play, period. Best practice is to carry a copy of the USGA's *The Rules of Golf* in your bag at all times.

Even though the rules seem very well spelled out, there's plenty of room for disagreement. When that happens, you either need to summon a rules official to adjudicate the situation, or play a second ball. For the sake of not slowing down the entire field, the best option is to play a second ball in addition to your original ball whenever possible.

For example: Bob accidentally kicked Terry's ball, which was lying in the rough. Terry's not sure what to do: Should he play it as it lies, or return the ball to the place from where it was kicked? Since they aren't sure how to proceed, the answer is for Terry to play it both ways. He plays the original ball as it lies after Bob kicked it; then he also plays a second ball from the spot where Bob kicked his original ball. He scores both balls. Then, at the end of the round, Bob and Terry check with the pro on which ball to score for Terry on that hole.

The second ball is a great way to avoid arguments on the course. Neither the player nor his opponent has to be "right." Use this concept to keep your focus on the game, and not on your opinion of your opponent's knowledge of the rules.

A Situation for a Rules Official

Mary and Sally are competing for the club championship. Mary's drive slices to the right and appears to land out-of-bounds. To avoid slowing down play, she chooses to hit a provisional ball. Sally accompanies Mary to the area where Mary's first tee shot went. They spy the ball between two out-of-bounds stakes. Mary stands behind one of the stakes, lines up the two stakes her ball is between, and breathes a sigh of relief: As far as she can see, a small sliver of her ball is still in bounds and, according to the rules, "A ball is *out-of-bounds* when all of it lies *out-of-bounds*."

Sally also takes a look and says, "Mary, I'm not sure if it's in or out, but the decision is up to you." By not directly challenging Mary's opinion about the position of her ball, Sally has taken the action that reflects the spirit of the game.

Mary's responsibility to the spirit of the game is to be absolutely certain she can see that at least part of her ball is still in bounds. If Mary simply can't be sure, she can ask if there's a rules official available to adjudicate the issue. One professional tells me that his staff does answer the call during tournaments to come out and decide issues such as the one confronting Mary. Each staff member carries a string to tie between the stakes, in order to determine if the ball is in or out-of-bounds. If, as can happen in a local tournament, there's no on-course official, then Mary herself has to decide what to do. Either the ball is in bounds or out-of-bounds. If she plays it as it lies, she's decided it was in bounds. If she plays the provisional ball, then she's decided the original ball was out-of-bounds.

IS IT OUT-OF-BOUNDS?

Situations like Mary's out-of-bounds dilemma arise more often than you might think. One way to resolve the issue without waiting for a rules official (see "A Situation for a Rules Official," page 150) is to carry a small ball of string in your bag. Have two people from your group hold the string on the inside edges of the out-of-bounds stakes on either side of the ball, then pull the string taut to form the out-of-bounds line. It then becomes easy to judge whether any part of the ball is "sliced" by the string. If it is, then the ball is in bounds; if it isn't, then it's out-of-bounds.

WATCH THE CHITCHAT

Often, in a tournament, you end up playing with strangers or with people you don't know well. While your regular group may enjoy your constant banter and stream of funny jokes, give it a rest on this day. The other competitors may want to focus more diligently on their game, and your talking could break their concentration.

A bigger problem arises when you end up playing with friends during a tournament. In this case, everybody knows one another, and your usual modus operandi is to have a good time. Today is a day to throttle it back, however. Don't put your pals in the difficult position of having to ask you to tone it down. You'll be doing them a favor, and you'll have the opportunity to focus on your game as well. It's a win-win solution for everyone.

WATCH YOUR MANNERS AROUND THE GREEN

Even though you always take care not to step on a person's line, and to mark your ball, and to do your part as far as piniquette is concerned, during a tournament you'll want to heighten your efforts on the green. Whereas in a friendly game you might . . .

- take a big step over a line . . . in a tournament, walk around the marker or the competitor's ball

- casually mark your ball . . . in a tournament, take special care to place the marker right behind your ball and to return the ball to exactly the same spot

- walk around the opposite side of the cup from a competitor's line . . . in a tournament, give the cup a wide berth so you don't walk where he might be putting if his first putt passes the cup

- pick up the flagstick while others are still putting . . . in a tournament, leave it on the ground until everyone is done putting; also, if it's windy and the flag is fluttering, gently hold the flag down with your foot

- just step up and tend the pin . . . in a tournament, be sure to first ask the person putting whether she wants the pin tended

TAKE SPECIAL CARE IN BUNKERS

Fred sometimes inadvertently touches the sand during the takeaway of a bunker shot—a rules violation. No one says anything in a friendly game, but in a tournament it could cause him trouble. The best thing I can do for Fred is to caution him about his indiscretion before the round begins: "Fred, just a word of caution. Sometimes in the bunker, you inadvertently let your club touch the sand on your backswing. Please be careful about that today, so no one calls you on it."

THE DILIGENT SCOREKEEPER

At the start of each round in a tournament, the starter will give each team or each competitor an opponent's scorecard. Because Harry is keeping Sam's score and vice versa, it becomes critical that they announce their scores to each other clearly at the end of each hole. In friendly games, we often assume the person scoring knows how we did. In my regular group, we're probably more cavalier about this than we should be. But in serious tournament play, make sure the person keeping your score knows what you had on each hole.

Tournament scorecards even have a row of boxes at the bottom of the card, which conveniently has a perforation just above it. As a check, Harry and Sam enter their own scores for each hole in that bottom row of boxes. At the end of the round, Harry tears off the score he has been keeping for himself, then places it right above the scores Sam has been keeping for him and makes sure their scores for each hole match. Sam does the same with the card Harry has been keeping for him. If there's any dispute, they can clear it up before they both sign and submit the card.

This cross-check is vitally important, because once the scorecard has been turned in, it cannot be changed. (See "The Stroke Shaver," page 117.)

The Tee Markers Matter

It seems pretty obvious that a player on the tee should tee his ball somewhere between the tee markers and not in front of the tee markers. But what happens if, in a tournament, a competitor inadvertently tees up his ball and hits it from just in front of the markers?

In stroke play, he must re-tee the ball, and he also incurs a two-stroke penalty, so his second drive is his third shot. Ouch!

In match play, there is no penalty. However, the opponent can make an immediate demand that the player hit a second tee shot from the correct position. From the point of view of gaining the most advantage over your opponent, if the first shot went out-of-bounds, or in a hazard, or was a duffed shot, you could opt to say nothing. But if it was a perfect drive up the middle, you may choose to demand that the player drive again.

In either format, the spirit of the game dictates that if you notice the error before the shot is taken, you must stop your competitor from hitting and point out that he's teed the ball outside the tee markers. "Hey, Bob, I don't know if you realized it, but you're teed up in front of the tee markers." This way, you avoid the delicate and difficult problem (at least in stroke play) of having to call him on the mistake after the fact.

For the Integrity of the Field: When It Doesn't Pay to Be the Nice Guy

In a stroke-play tournament, your opponent, Jack, lies three before he makes a shot out of a bunker. You notice that on his backswing, his club clearly touches the sand—a violation of play in a hazard (see "Take Special Care in Bunkers," page 152).

THE SANDBAGGER ISN'T ALWAYS A SANDBAGGER

Nothing frustrates golfers more than competing against a sandbagger in a tournament. The sandbagger falsifies scores so that his handicap is higher than it should be, and then has an edge in the tournament because he's really a better player than his handicap says he is. In a match-play tournament, he ends up with extra strokes that he doesn't deserve.

I've been in match-play tournaments where the sandbagger walks away with the trophy and everyone else is left with a bad taste in their mouths. But sometimes the sandbagger isn't really a sandbagger. Sometimes he's just an ordinary golfer who has a great day. I'm a 17 handicapper, but one year, playing in the second flight, I went on a tear on the final day, shooting a 79 to win my division.

The only time consideration of sandbagging should be raised is when the player seems to score much better than his handicap repeatedly, in tournament after tournament. That's when a tournament committee or the professional running the event should consider adjusting the player's handicap before the tournament starts.

Do you say anything? "Maybe I'll just mention it to him quietly," you think. You do, and he thanks you. That's a mistake, because now you're both making a choice not to follow a rule of golf, which is itself against the rules. Trying to be the nice guy in this way doesn't pay.

The fact is, golfers in a tournament have a responsibility to uphold the rules for the integrity of the entire field of competitors. Not calling Bob on his misstep affects everyone in the tournament. You really have no choice: Point out the infraction to Jack. He now lies five, not four.

Hitting Out of Turn Can Be Costly

How costly? Just ask Annika Sorenstam. During the 2000 Solheim Cup tournament, a match-play event, Annika holed a beautiful chip shot on the thirteenth hole at the Loch Lomond Golf Club in Scotland. Unfortunately, she had played out of turn. Interestingly, the Americans consulted with their captain, Pat Bradley, who took the matter into her own hands and made the decision to require that Annika replay the shot in her proper turn. Needless to say, Annika didn't repeat the holed chip shot.

Although, as team captain, Bradley was perfectly within her rights to ask Annika to replay the shot, there was some controversy over the decision because some people thought it violated the spirit of the game.

The One Time That Practice May Not Make Perfect

The rules permit you to take a practice putt during a round after you hole out, but before you decide to do so, be sure to check whether there's a local rule prohibiting practice putts during a round. Once you've checked for any local rules, as a matter of etiquette, take a look around you before you drop a ball on the green, to be sure your practice doesn't hold up the play of the group behind you.

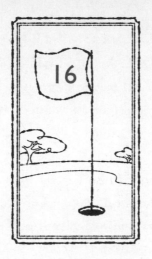

PLAYING FOR "A LITTLE SOMETHING"

HE USUAL?" IS A QUESTION MOST COMMONLY HEARD AT A BAR, BUT IT APPLIES EQUALLY TO FOURSOMES GATHERING FOR THEIR WEEKLY GOLF GAME. Usually, the "usual" is a Nassau (see "The King of Golf Games: The Nassau," page 164), a little golf betting game that participants believe makes the game of golf more interesting. The world of betting on golf has its own guidelines, which serve to keep the game fair for everyone involved. Knowing these guidelines is important: If you run afoul of them, your reputation will suffer and your relationships may evaporate. On a personal level, that would be frustrating. And if you're playing business golf, such a misstep could be very expensive, indeed.

FIVE GUIDELINES WHEN YOU'RE PLAYING FOR A LITTLE SOMETHING

If you're going to participate in a contest where there's "a little something" at stake, there are a few important tenets you should be aware of.

1. Pay Your Bets

In an interview with *Time* magazine, Lee Trevino famously commented, "A $5 bet and only $2 in your pocket—that's pressure." Don't bet if you can't pay up.

2. Know the Details Before You Jump In

Ralph was visiting Las Vegas a couple of years ago and had some time on his hands. So he went to one of the nearby courses and ended up picking up a game with three locals. On the first tee, the three locals began the chatter with that familiar question: "The usual?" They picked teams and commenced play. Soon, Ralph discovered that he was playing with two casino owners and a casino general manager. The sweat started beading on his forehead as he began to wonder just what the usual bet was. Finally, at the sixth tee, he couldn't stand it any longer. He turned to his partner and, in the most casual tone he could muster, asked, "So, just what is the usual?"

"A one-dollar Nassau. Why?" came the reply.

3. Don't Coerce Fellow Golfers Into Participating

First and foremost, it's important to point out that no person should ever be coerced into participating in a contest involving betting. One member of our foursome, for example, hit a bad stretch with his game at one point. Betting just added to his un-happiness; not only was he frustrated with himself, but he was also feeling guilty at not supporting his partner that week. One day he simply said, "You guys go ahead and play a game. But I'm not interested." We didn't needle him; we honored his request, and found an alternative game to play among the three of us.

4. Be Honest About Your Handicap

The sandbagger is frustrating when he's a stranger. When he's a friend, a regular, people likely won't want to play with him for long, since nobody appreciates being taken advantage of. What's more, everyone knows just what type of game the other members of their foursome play—so nobody's fooling anybody if they try to claim a higher handicap than they're due.

5. Who Buys the Drinks?

While some may think it's a tradition for the winner to buy the drinks, it's not. It is the winner's (or loser's) *prerogative* to offer to buy drinks.

THE HANDICAP SYSTEM

This system, also known as handicapping, is how golf equalizes the game between people of different skill levels. The handicap system makes it possible for golfers of different abilities to compete on equal footing with each other.

Here's how it works: Each golfer who wants to compete, be it in a serious tournament like a club championship or in a friendly Saturday-morning Nassau (see "The King of Golf Games: The Nassau," page 164), records the score for each round he or she plays. Typically, the scores are recorded on a computer at your club. (The club pro shop will tell you how to get a member number that you can use to record your scores.) Once every couple of weeks, the members' handicaps will be updated to reflect the latest scores. Essentially, your handicap is determined by averaging the best ten scores of your last twenty rounds. It's a little more complicated than this, but that's the basic idea.

FULL OR NET HANDICAP?

There are two ways to equalize handicaps: Each player gets all the strokes due him—full handicap—or the group "plays off" the person with the lowest handicap.

Full Handicap Method

Some groups will play with a full handicap, meaning that each person gets as many strokes as their handicap. On any hole a player gets a stroke, he deducts one stroke from his score on that hole. For instance, a 5 becomes a 4 or a 4 becomes a 3. A 2-handicap golfer would get a stroke on the number one and two handicap holes (the two-toughest holes) as listed on the scorecard. If she's playing a 6-handicap golfer, then Six would get strokes on the top-six-hardest handicap holes. That means that Six would have a stroke advantage over Two on the third-hardest through sixth-hardest handicap holes (*not* the first through fourth handicap holes).

Playing Off the Lowest Golfer's Handicap

If, on the other hand, Two and Six opted to play off Two's handicap, then Six would get strokes on the first, second, third, and fourth handicap holes, and Two would get no strokes.

The difference between these two approaches really boils down to a question of which hole(s) the stroke differential is awarded on, based on the handicap on the course. Most people play off the low handicap golfer's handicap, so that the advantage is given on the harder handicap holes. Regardless of how the group you're in does it, check carefully ahead of time, so that if you get strokes, you'll know which holes you're getting them on.

If you are doing the scoring, it's most courteous to announce who gets strokes on a particular hole *at the start of the hole.* Certainly, this approach is more in the spirit of the game than hoping your competitor doesn't realize he had a stroke advantage on that hole and then telling him about it at the end of the hole. This knowledge could matter. Suppose, for example, that Two says nothing to Six on the fourth-hardest hole, where Six has a stroke advantage. Two sinks a long putt for a par, and Six lies five feet from the cup. Six doesn't realize she's still in the hole since, if she sinks her putt for a 5, she'll tie Two with a net 4. Instead of putting, Six figures she's lost the hole so she picks up her ball and walks off the green. Big mistake.

It's a lost opportunity for Six, and when she realizes what happened she won't be very happy with Two. Of course, if this happened in a friendly game, the polite thing for Two to do would be to offer Six a chance to replace the ball and attempt the putt.

LISTEN UP CAREFULLY

Despite all the rules for all the games and side bets, everything is negotiable. You may run into groups that do a lot of negotiating. When you do, listen carefully, stick up for your own rights, and be sure you understand any and all variations before accepting the bet. For example, typically, the people I play with play to full handicaps. Occasionally, however, you may link up with a group where they take only 80 percent of each person's handicap. For example, a 10-handicap golfer would only get eight strokes. As long as it's done equitably, no harm, no foul.

FYI: MATCH PLAY VS. STROKE PLAY

Golf can be played with each competitor's total score being compared to all the other competitors' scores. That's called stroke play. Alternatively, in match play, two individuals or teams compete on a hole-by-hole basis. Both formats make for great competition, but which one your group chooses to play can have an effect on the final outcome of the match—as you're about to see.

Match Play

Leah and Stephanie have a nine-hole match. They share the same handicap, so there are no strokes given to either player. Leah wins the first two holes. In golf-speak, Leah is now two up—or Stephanie can think of herself as two down. Stephanie wins the next three holes. Now Stephanie is one up, while Leah thinks of herself as one down. They tie the next three holes. After eight holes,

Stephanie is still one up with one hole to play. That means she can't lose, since the best Leah can do is tie her by winning the last hole. In golf-speak, Stephanie is "dormie" because she cannot lose the match. As it happens, they tie the last hole, so Stephanie, still one up, wins the match outright.

Hole	1	2	3	4	5	6	7	8	9	
Par	4	4	3	5	4	4	3	4	5	
Leah	4	5	4	6	5	7	4	5	6	46
Stephanie	7	8	3	5	4	7	4	5	6	49
	+1	+2	+1	0	-1	-1	-1	-1	-1	

Stroke Play

In stroke play, the only thing that matters is the total score at the end of the match. In Leah and Stephanie's contest, if they were playing stroke play, the outcome would have been different. Leah kept score, so the card is written from her perspective. Leah loses if the contest is match play, but wins if it's stroke play.

THE GAMES GOLFERS PLAY

There are many games that golfers play, and many variations on these games. A few, however, seem universal in their appeal. By searching the Internet using the phrase "golf betting games," you can find numerous Web sites explaining these games and their variations, as well as many other lesser-known games. For the knowledgeable golfer, these explanations are a helpful refresher. For the new golfer, an understanding of these games means that he or she can stand on the first tee with at least some idea of how to play the game of the day.

The King of Golf Games: The Nassau

The Nassau is the most likely "usual" game. Usually, it's played in a match-play format, although it can be played as a stroke-play contest. It's really three separate games, played between two individuals or two teams. The first game is for which team wins the front nine. The second game is for which team wins the back nine. The third game is for which team wins the full eighteen holes.

How it works: Typically, there's a separate bet for each game. Often one golfer will suggest, "Is two, two, two okay with everybody?" This simply means that the bet on the front nine is for $2, the back nine bet is for $2, and the eighteen-hole bet is for $2. If a team loses all three bets, each team member is on the hook to pay $6 to a member of the winning team. "Two, two, five" would mean that the front and back nine bets are $2 each, while the eighteen-hole match is for $5.

Be sure you know the dollar amount for the game that day, especially if you're playing with strangers. Their "two, two, two" could be for $200 instead of $2. So be careful.

The Press

The most common addition to the Nassau is "the press." A press initiates another bet for the rest of that nine or for the rest of the eighteen holes. The most typical press is the two-down press: After two holes, Stephanie (remember her?) finds herself down two. If they're playing a Nassau and playing the two-down press option, since she's two down, she could press (or "challenge") Leah to another bet before starting play on the third hole. The terms typically are the same as for the original bet.

Some groups will have a rule that all presses must be accepted, while others will let the side being pressed decide whether to accept or decline the press. That said, declining a press is rarely done. If Leah accepts the press, an additional new bet starts on the third hole.

Be careful with presses: They can get expensive quickly, especially if your group allows automatic presses. Automatic presses occur as soon as a trigger point is reached. In Stephanie and Leah's match, for example, an automatic press would have kicked in as soon as Leah won the second hole. Over an eighteen-hole match, several presses could happen.

Junk or Dings

Junk bets, also known as "dings," are additional payouts for certain accomplishments on the course. The bet might call for $1 per junk payout. In a team event, if the agreed amount for junk is $1, this means $1 per person. So if Doug is my partner and I get a sandie (see below), we'll each get a dollar from the other team. There are dozens of possibilities for junk bets. Again, if you want a list of ideas, you can go online and find numerous sites that explain junk bets. Here are four of the most common.

> *Sandies.* Play a sand shot out of a bunker and then sink the next shot for a par score on that hole.
>
> *Greenies.* On a par 3, your tee shot lands on the green and you then make par. If two or more players land on

the green, only the player closest to the pin can win the greenie on that hole. Some groups will carry forward greenies if no one wins a given hole. By the third or fourth par 3, the greenie can triple or quadruple in value, making for a tasty payout.

Birdies. Make one under par on a hole.

Barkies. Hit a tree and still make par on a hole.

Agreement on which junk will be counted should be made before the round commences. If you're not sure, simply ask, "Any junk today?"

Skins

Skins became popularized when the Skins Game was televised for the first time on Thanksgiving weekend in 1983, with Gary Player winning the inaugural event. The format is simple. Even better, it doesn't require a foursome to play, so it's a good alternative when one of your foursome can't make it to your weekly game.

How it works: Players agree on a certain value per hole for each player for the round. For example, Bill, Doug, and Peter agree to play for $1 a hole. This means that each hole is worth $3 and that the most any golfer will be out-of-pocket at the end of the round is $18. (Remember: Always know what the game is and the amount you're in for *before* agreeing to play.)

Whoever wins a hole wins the money pool for the hole. If two or more players tie, the money carries over to the next hole. (Some golfers may choose not play the carry-forward option, but instead will cancel the bet on that hole.)

One variation, which the Skins Game on television employs,

is to up the dollar amount after the sixth and twelfth holes. In this variation, Bill, Doug, and Peter could have agreed to play for $1 for the first six holes, $1.50 for the next six holes, and $2 for the last six holes. In that case, the total value of the bet per person would be $27.

If no one wins the final hole, the group may decide to not award that skin and any cumulative skins accompanying that hole. Or they may decide to have a play-off, probably on the putting green.

5-3-1, or Baseball

Baseball is a perfect threesome game. How it works: Players accumulate points on each hole. The rules are simple. Let's say Maureen, Leigh, and Tricia decide to play Baseball. On each hole, a total of 9 points are allocated, with 5 points awarded for coming in first, 3 points for second, and 1 for third. Ties split the points evenly. If all three players tie on a hole, each gets 3 points. Their scorecard might look like this:

Hole	1	2	3	4	5	6	7	8	9	
Par	4	4	3	4	5	4	5	3	4	
Maureen	4	5	4	4	7	4	6	4	5	43
Leigh	4	6	4	5	5	4	6	3	5	42
Tricia	5	4	4	4	6	4	6	3	5	41

Maureen	4	3	3	4	1	3	3	1	3	25
Leigh	4	1	3	1	5	3	3	4	3	27
Tricia	1	5	3	4	3	3	3	4	3	29

Hole	10	11	12	13	14	15	16	17	18	
Par	3	4	4	4	3	4	4	4	5	
Maureen	3	6	5	5	4	5	5	4	4	41
Leigh	4	4	5	6	3	5	4	5	5	41
Tricia	4	5	6	5	3	5	4	5	6	43
Maureen	5	1	4	4	1	3	1	5	5	29
Leigh	2	5	4	1	4	3	4	2	3	28
Tricia	2	3	1	4	4	3	4	2	1	24

The top three rows show their scores; the bottom three rows show how the bet scored. Maureen ends up with 54 points, Leigh with 55 points, and Tricia with 53 points. If they're playing for $1 per point, Tricia ends up paying Leigh $2 and Maureen $1, while Maureen pays Leigh $1.

Wolf

Wolf adds spice to a golf round, since on any given hole you may end up partnered with a different golfer in the foursome. Wolf also requires whoever is the wolf to assess the skills and perhaps consider who gets strokes on which hole. While it can be played with four players, it's an especially great threesome game.

How it works: At the start of the round, Doug, Bill, and Peter toss tees or use some other random process to assign the tee-off order. The order then rotates on each successive hole. Doug wins the toss, so he's the wolf on the first hole, the fourth hole, and so on. Peter is second, so he's the wolf on the second hole, the fifth hole, and so on. Bill is wolf on the remaining holes. The wolf always tees off last, while the other two players use the honors method to determine their order of play (see "Wait Up!" page 22).

On the first hole, Peter tees off first. Before Bill drives, Doug, the wolf, must decide if he wants to choose Peter as a partner for the hole. He doesn't like Peter's drive, so he doesn't choose Peter. Once Bill drives, there's no going back to claim Peter as a partner. Doug then assesses Bill's drive and decides whether he wants Bill as a partner, or prefers to go it alone. Because Bill has hit an awesome drive, Doug decides to partner with Bill.

So now the game is on, with Peter playing a one-hole best-ball match against the team of Doug—the wolf—and Bill. If Doug and Bill's best ball beats Peter's, they're each awarded one point. If they tie, no points are awarded. If Peter wins, then he's awarded one point.

If Doug, as the wolf, decides to go it alone, he would be competing against the team of Peter and Bill. If Doug wins, he gets two points. If it's a tie, as the wolf Doug gets one point. If he loses, Peter and Bill each get one point.

Points are totaled at the end of the round. The points are assigned a dollar value, and the bet is then paid off. One variation is to double the points on a hole if the wolf goes it alone. Another variation is to triple the points on a hole if the wolf announces before anyone tees off that he's going it alone.

ACCEPTABILITY OF WAGERING

"A little something" adds spice to the game and creates an outlet for people who like to compete. It's important to reiterate, however, that it's patently unacceptable to coerce or badger another person in your foursome into taking part in a bet. Likewise, it's unacceptable for any golfer to enter into a bet they don't want to take part in or can't comfortably afford. If you don't want to bet, don't feel coerced into doing it. The other golfers have plenty of options. If you do join the bet, know the game, know the amounts, and be prepared to pay up as soon as the round is over.

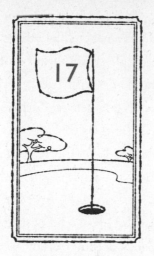

DON'T WE ALL WISH THAT PRACTICE MADE PERFECT?

THE PRACTICE AREA IS A PLACE WHERE GOLFERS CAN GREET ONE ANOTHER, SHARE A STORY OR TWO, MAKE PLANS TO PLAY GOLF OR WHATEVER, GIVE ONE ANOTHER TIPS ON HOW TO IMPROVE THEIR SWINGS, EVEN TRY TO CONCENTRATE ON A LESSON WITH ONE OF THE CLUB'S GOLF PROFESSIONALS. In essence, it's social golf—only not with just a foursome, but with a multitude of golfers. Therefore, it's a place where all the issues of safety and etiquette are magnified exponentially.

SOCIAL GOLF: THE PRACTICE AREA

The social aspect of golf may be the most important aspect of the game for many golfers. Yes, they'd like to score well—but deep down, they know they're never likely to be as good a golfer as they'd like. They accept this dichotomy because the real pleasure comes from enjoying being with friends, meeting new people, and building business relationships. The performance aspect of golf becomes a catalyst for the social aspect of the game.

While the camaraderie of the foursome is the nucleus of social golf, the practice area can put ten, twelve, or even thirty or forty golfers together in one place. And my experience is that if you do that, you're bound to get a lot of socializing.

Intrinsically, there's nothing wrong with socializing in the practice area if it's done with some consideration for the golfers around you who are actually working on their games.

Chitchat

More than once I've observed the following situation.

It's Saturday morning and golfers are flocking to the course. The practice area is full and a few golfers are hanging nearby, waiting patiently. Dan is in the middle of his practice session when his good buddy, Mike, arrives. Mike has had an awesome evening the night before, and he can't wait to tell Dan about it.

Mike walks down the practice line to Dan's position. Dan turns to greet his friend, maybe even shake his hand; then Mike launches into a description of what he did last night. Yak, yak, yak. (For some reason, even the most taciturn of people can run at the mouth with the best of them once they have a golf club in their hands.)

Bill, who's been waiting patiently for his turn at the practice tee, starts to get a little steamed. Why? Because suddenly Dan and Mike are taking up space at a station, but neither of them is practicing.

Greeting a fellow golfer at a practice station is one thing. Blocking others from using the station while you're having a conversation and not using it yourself is unacceptable.

SAFETY IN THE PRACTICE AREA

While Mike and Dan are talking, their focus is on their conversation and not necessarily on the activity going on around them. Mike's a pretty effusive guy. When he talks, he gestures, and he simply can't stand still. At the next station, Fred is starting to practice. He brings out his new 46-inch, 460-cubic-centimeter,

man-size driver and takes one step back from his teed-up ball for his first practice swing with this powerful new weapon. Mike feels a sudden gust of wind as the head of Fred's driver tickles the hairs growing on the edge of his right ear.

Disaster has been averted—but only by sheer luck.

Here are some smart safety guidelines for the practice area.

One person at a time at or near a station. The exception is when you're working with a pro, in which case the station next to you and the pro should be empty.

Stay in the hitting area. Never wander forward to get a duffed ball or a tee, or try practicing off the grass instead of the mat.

Clear the area before leaving. Whether you're stepping back to get a club, or you've finished your practice and are ready to leave, before moving, you should look to both sides to make sure an adjacent golfer can't hit you with his swing. Remember, too, that even if you're at a safe distance, the golfer at the next station may see your movement in his backswing and screw up the shot. If your neighbor is in mid-swing, give him a chance to finish before departing; it's only a matter of seconds.

THE PUTTING GREEN

Like the practice area, the putting green often has several people on it. Being considerate of the other people on the green involves a few commonsense guidelines.

KIDS AND PRACTICE

Nothing frightens me more than to see a practice area with one or two young kids hitting golf balls and running around unsupervised by an adult. They seem to move from one potential disaster to the next, and it's only by sheer luck that nothing untoward happens. Do not use the practice area or putting green as a play area for your children. The consequences of being hit by a ball or a club are too serious.

"That's *My* Hole!"

Before a regular game, the practice green normally won't be too crowded. If it isn't, avoid putting to the same hole that another person is putting to. If the green is crowded, before hitting to the same hole that someone else is already hitting to, you might wait until he's finished, or ask first whether he minds.

Before a shotgun start (in which teams tee off on all eighteen holes simultaneously), the practice green could easily have thirty or more golfers on it. Even in this situation, you should be careful about putting to a hole that someone else is putting to. Until a hole opens up, consider placing a tee on the surface and putting to it, or picking an old hole mark and putting to it. Also, as you're walking across the green, take care not to step in front of another person's putt and have it hit your foot.

The Rocket Flop Shot

Perhaps my greatest fear on the practice green is the reckless person who's trying to hit full-swing, high flop shots to the practice green. It's not that trying to work on this shot is wrong—in fact, I've done it myself. But because this is a shot that can easily be bladed, before I attempt it, I always make sure that there's nobody across from me who I might hit if I rocket an attempted flop shot across the green at waist height.

"Those Are My Balls!"

One fine spring day, Paul approached the practice green and spied Bob, who had just finished rounding up some balls to practice chipping with. Paul promptly reached out his pitching wedge and pulled away a few of the balls from Bob's pile. Bob saw the action out of the corner of his eye and was flabbergasted. "Hey," he thought, "I spent a couple of minutes collecting those balls. The least he could do is to ask before taking them."

Aloud to Paul, he said sarcastically, "Go ahead—take all you want. I'll get more." The situation went downhill from there.

Bottom line: Paul's action was unacceptable. Whether you're on the putting green or in the practice area, you don't take practice balls that someone else is working from without asking first. On the other side of the coin, once the faux pas was committed, Bob's reply was a bit caustic. A less accusatory approach would have been better. Sometimes the best thing to do is to say or do nothing. In this case, ignoring the faux pas would have been a better course of action.

THE NINETEENTH HOLE

EPENDING ON THE KIND OF GAME I'VE HAD, THIS MAY BE THE BEST PART OF THE DAY. It can be a place to celebrate a great round, or a place to assuage my sorrows. Best of all, however, it's a place to spend a few minutes of time socializing with my foursome and with any other golfers who happen to be there. I'm referring, of course, to the nineteenth hole—the bar/restaurant that can be found at almost every golf course or golf club. It's a great setting for cementing relationships, meeting new people, and even making a little headway on that business you wanted to conduct. Following are a few guidelines to help ensure that this special place is everything to you that it should be.

ALWAYS PAY YOUR BETS

Always settle your bets promptly. Best time to pay up: either as you're walking back to the pro shop after the round, or once all the tabulating is done at the nineteenth hole. If you were playing with your boss and he lost, don't make a big deal of it by saying, "Hey, Boss, you owe me $6." But when (and it should always be "when," not "if") he offers, graciously accept your winnings. Don't say, "Oh, Boss, that's not necessary." Needless to say, if you owe the boss, be sure to pay up right away.

AN EMPTY SEAT AT THE TABLE

As Cy's foursome walks off the eighteenth green, Tim turns to Cy and the others and says, "That was fun, but I gotta run. See you guys next week." For Tim, his premature departure is disappointing, to be sure. The chance to share a libation, alcoholic or otherwise, and maybe a bite to eat, and to relive the round and shoot the breeze for half an hour is lost. It's a letdown for the rest of his foursome, as well. The post-round get-together is an important part of the social aspect of the game that golfers cherish, and when one golfer bails out, it's just as disappointing to the others as it is to the bailer. For this reason, you should always try to plan your golf schedule to include not only time for the game itself, but also fifteen minutes to half an hour for socializing after the round.

 Business Golf Tip

Getting Business Done

If this has been a business outing and you're the host/organizer, the nineteenth hole presents an opportunity for you to bring up the business subject at hand. Rather than making a full-blown proposal, however, treat this time as an opportunity to set up an appointment with your prospect/guest to discuss the matter further.

Conversely, if you're the one who's been invited on the outing, this is a great time to offer your thanks for an awesome round of golf and even offer to buy a round of drinks. If your host hasn't mentioned business, this is also the time to let him know that if there's anything you can do for him, you'd be pleased to meet at a later time to discuss his needs. If he takes the bait, great. If not, let it pass. You can always phone him the next day to thank him again, and use that phone call to address any business ideas or issues you wanted to bring up.

WHO BUYS THE DRINKS?

As John and Paul leave the green, their wallets are a little heavier, thanks to the $8 in winnings they've each just pocketed. Larry and Randy are acquaintances who had joined them for the round, and things had gotten a little competitive back on thirteen when the press was made—so the fact that they'd won the press on the last hole was especially sweet. Unfortunately, that sweet sensation is punctured when, from behind them, Larry's voice pipes up, "Thanks guys. By the way, winners buy the drinks."

John stops in his tracks. *What?* he thinks. "Let's get this straight—I win eight dollars, and now I'm expected to shell out eight dollars, ten dollars, or twelve dollars or more for a couple of drinks?"

What makes it particularly galling is that the drinks challenge was tossed out after the round was over, rather than before it started. While in fact John had been planning to offer to buy drinks, now there was no chance he was going to fall into Larry's trap. It simply isn't obligatory that winners buy drinks at the nineteenth hole. The reality is if people are buying rounds, *all* the members of a foursome should participate—although, in the interests of safe driving, not necessarily on the same day.

YOUR MONEY'S NO GOOD HERE

Some clubs only allow food and drink to be paid for by charging it to a member's account. This means that, as a guest, you won't be able to put a round of drinks on your tab. Instead—as with your round of golf, any caddie fees, and any other incidental expenses—be sure to offer to reimburse your host. He may decline, but you should still make the offer.

TIPPING

The staff at the nineteenth hole is just as important as the backroom boys and the golf staff. If you're at a club that adds the gratuity to the bill, handing out an additional tip once in a while is a great way to let the person who serves you regularly, or is at the bar every week when your group comes in, know that you appreciate the service you receive. If your club doesn't add the gratuity to the tab automatically, pay the tip yourself (it should be at least 15 to 20 percent of the total bill, before taxes), and consider giving a little extra once in a while to the staff member who's your "regular," or who makes an extra effort for you. Remember, tips are a means of showing appreciation for service rendered.

TIPS ON TIPPING

Around the club, you will run into a variety of people to whom it may be appropriate to offer a tip. The amounts listed are guidelines and can vary from club to club. If you're not sure, ask for guidance. These include:

- Backroom boys: $2–$5 per service, or make a contribution to the annual backroom boys tip fund.

- Caddies: $25–$50.

- Starter: $5 every now and then, or have your group put $5 per person together occasionally and give it to him as a group tip.

- Bartenders: $1–$5, or a larger tip once in a while for a regular. One golfer gives his winnings to the bartender, but he doesn't ask for a refund when he loses.

- Waitstaff: While gratuities are often included in food bills, you can opt to give an extra $5 tip to the waitperson who regularly takes care of you or who makes a special effort on your group's behalf. Again, the group tip could work well here.

- Locker-room attendants (for shining shoes or other efforts on your behalf): $5.

THE LOCKER ROOM

You might use the facilities at the club to change into your street clothes after your round, and perhaps even shower and shave. If you do, respect the other members by making sure to clean up after yourself before leaving: towels in the towel bin, sink rinsed out, waste thrown away.

"FUN" GOLF VS. "SERIOUS" GOLF: WHEN TO CUT SOME SLACK

EVERY DAY, GOLFERS TEE IT UP SOMEWHERE. They meet on the first tee, decide what game, if any, they will play, and toss balls or tees to see who goes first. Then the fun begins. It's not a tournament; it's the weekly game. Or maybe you're a single, picking up a game and looking to meet some people. Or perhaps you're out with your significant other, or your daughter or son. Who knows? But underneath it all is the simple desire to enjoy yourself. Sure you want to play well, but you also want to have fun. Throughout this book, comments by survey respondents reinforce this notion that golf is really the catalyst for having a good time. And when that good time is marred by the travails of a fellow golfer who's off his game, it's time to make an adjustment—even if this means bending the rules.

"BUT THAT'S NOT THE USGA WAY!"

I fully understand that the advice in this chapter could be objectionable to the USGA or to golf purists. The reality, however, is that what I'm describing as "fun" golf—in which golfers take non-USGA sanctioned relief, yet still record their scores for handicap purposes—is the way 98 percent of golfers play golf with their regular groups. For the beginner, it can be incredibly confusing to be told first to follow the rules at all times, and then to see golfers taking liberties. They think: "Is bending this rule okay? Can I do that? What *can* I do?" This chapter will attempt to clarify that confusion. Relief happens. Bending of the rules happens. And as long as it is done just within the group in the context of "fun" golf, it will continue to happen. Bottom line: Stop having angst and feeling guilty, and start enjoying the game.

THE SPIRIT OF THE NO-FOUR-PUTT RULE

Wait a minute, you say—you have your rulebook in hand, and nowhere do you see anything about a "No-Four-Putt Rule."

Correct.

In fact, this rule most certainly violates the USGA's *The Rules of Golf* for stroke play. In a stroke-play tournament, failure to hole out disqualifies you—and so, in a stroke-play tournament, you hole out.

But what about stroke play when you're playing by yourself, or playing for "a little something" on a stroke-play basis? Say you and your opponent have one-footers and the group behind is waiting impatiently. Ninety-nine out of 100 times, it's "good/good" and on to the next tee. That's collusion, too: Now you're in real trouble with the USGA! The point is that we give relief in spite of the rules. What this means is that even in "handicap rounds," it's not a matter of *if golfers give relief*, but rather a matter of *what relief we'll give.*

The No-Four-Putt Rule is a prime example of bending the rules to pay homage to the importance of preserving the "fun" of the game for everyone. It's Doug's rule, or at least he initiated me into it. The spirit of the No-Four-Putt Rule is an outgrowth of the near-universal experience of a golfer who's having a horrendous putting day, and the impact that experience invariably has on the other golfers in the foursome—as well as, incidentally, its impact on the pace of play.

The Four-Putting Golfer

It's pretty certain that a golfer who faces a fourth putt is going to have a little black cloud start to form over his head. A couple of more four-putt holes, and that black cloud can quickly become a category 5 hurricane (see Chapter 12, " 'Son, You're Not Good Enough to Throw Clubs,' " pages 122–131). Is it worth adhering to the letter of the rules, only to watch him self-destruct for the rest of the round? Clearly, it isn't. And so out comes the "No-Four-Putt Rule," and perhaps the sun can start shining for this unfortunate individual once again.

Do It for the Rest of the Group

Too many times, I've had the unpleasant experience of playing with someone whose game has fallen apart. It doesn't matter where the problem is occurring—on the green, the fairway, the bunkers, or the tee box. Wherever and whenever it happens, it's painful to watch. You find yourself wanting to do or say almost anything to alleviate your companion's pain and allow the fun to return: "Take a mulligan." "Pick it up and toss it out of the trap." "That's good," when the golfer is facing a ten-foot putt.

At this point, his suffering is affecting you and the others in your group. Not only is his darkening mood a problem, but, frankly, when I play with someone whose game is in the tank it also tends to start affecting my game as well. I know, it shouldn't— mental toughness and all. But it does. And if, by bending the rules a bit, I can give him a little relief and get some for my game at the same time, so be it.

Do It to Avoid Slow Play

Besides the negative effect on everyone's psyche, when you make a struggling golfer keep putting, or continue to hit balls wildly off the tee instead dropping one out in the fairway, or keep flailing in the sand instead of using a hand mashie, it also lengthens the time it takes to complete a hole. Now his bad day is affecting not only him and the rest of your group, but the golfers behind you as well.

How to Employ the No-Four-Putt Rule

As with other changes, any change to the rules should be agreed upon by the entire group at the start of the round. In our group, the only other way the No-Four-Putt Rule possibly might be instituted is when the situation first crops up on a green (i.e., one of the group three-putts and still hasn't put his ball in the cup), and one of the other players simply says, "Let's not let anyone four-putt today."

If a four-putt situation arises and the No-Four-Putt Rule has already been mentioned on the first tee, then another player should probably reiterate the earlier decision by saying, "No four putts today; pick it up." The person putting shouldn't call the rule for himself, just as he doesn't roll the ball out of a divot himself, but instead waits for another player to suggest it.

Once established, the rule is good for the round—meaning that in all subsequent instances, the third putt is automatically good, no matter whose putt it is or how long it is, and it can either be picked up or putted for the practice.

OTHER "NO-FOUR-PUTT RULES"

Besides the No-Four-Putt Rule, there are a variety of other ways to offer relief when playing a "fun" round of golf. Here are some of the most popular.

> *Gimme.* The most common type of relief, the gimme, is most often given if the putt is "inside the leather." Take a standard putter and put the head gently in the hole. If the ball is no farther away than the start of the grip on the shaft, then the putt is conceded as "good." If someone gives you a putt, pick it up; don't putt it, at least not until after the hole is completed—at which point you can try it as a practice putt if no one is waiting behind you.

Lift, clean, and place. This one is just what it says: Mark the location of the ball; pick it up and clean it off; then replace it. In a friendly game, replace it close to the original position but not closer to the hole than the original lie, and don't move it to better conditions, such as from the rough into the fairway.

Divot relief. For the unlucky shot that finds its way into a divot, roll the ball just out of the divot so you can play it off the fairway.

The leaf ball. In the northern United States during the autumn months, fallen leaves, especially in the rough, can hide a ball unmercifully. You know the ball's right there, but no matter how hard you look or shuffle around, you'll never find it. With the approval of the other golfers in your group, drop another ball and play on.

Mulligan and roving mulligan. In essence, this is a do-over, typically of a tee shot. Most often, a mulligan is allowed on the first tee only. Some golfers, however, will play one mulligan per round, which can be taken on any tee. Others play the most liberal mulligan policy of all, which would give you a do-over anywhere on the course. Be careful, though, if you're last to hit on the first tee and no one else has taken a mulligan. After you hit a poor tee shot, don't simply announce that you're taking a mulligan and reach into your pocket for another ball. Instead, get the rules straight before anyone hits.

WHAT CONSTITUTES A GOOD TIME?

Think carefully for a moment about what you can do to contribute to a good time for everyone during a regular, non-serious, non-tournament outing.

Define your game at the start. Sometimes we want to bear down and play strictly by-the-rules golf. In preparation for a tournament, for example, it's sink-every-putt time. If you want to up the ante compared to your group's regular outings, where liberties may be taken, say so on the first hole, so everyone is on board at the outset.

Don't cheat. (See "When Is a Rule Bender a Cheat?" page 189.)

Leave work behind. This is a time to enjoy one another's company, not solve workplace issues. Think of your golf time as an opportunity to get away from work and clear your head. Maybe the issues will seem more manageable when you return to them later.

Encourage and compliment. Sincere encouragement and heartfelt compliments are appreciated. Be careful not to praise every shot, however. Comment occasionally, when it's really warranted.

RELIEF ONLY DURING NON-HANDICAP ROUNDS?

If we played strictly by the rules, we'd never enter a score from our weekly Thursday round. Of course, the USGA, or even some golfers, will point out that the rules don't ever permit one golfer to give relief to another in violation of the rules. They may even argue that such relief invalidates my score, and I can't enter it for my handicap. And, technically, they're right. Of course, if we followed their counsel, I probably wouldn't *have* a handicap, and neither would most golfers everywhere, because I'm sure that in every round I keep score on, there's at least one gimme or mulligan.

Who's really hurt as the result of this breaking of the rules? Me.

Here's why: Because of the relief I've been given, I put in a score that's lower than I probably would have gotten otherwise. And maybe that one-stroke-lower score was just the margin I needed to drop my handicap from 17 to 16. So next week, when I'm on the tee, I'll have to play to a 16 and get one less stroke from Doug, Dave, or Peter.

WHEN IS A RULE BENDER A CHEAT?

The difference between bending the rules and cheating is that the cheat is trying to gain an advantage over an opponent. In fun golf, all of the players are in on the "relaxing" of a rule and accept the advantage it may give a person. On more than one occasion, for instance, I'll come upon my ball lying in a deep divot on the fairway. All of a sudden, from across the fairway, I'll hear my opponent in the Nassau say, "Roll it, Peter." Now, if nothing had been said, I'd play it as it lay, because my moving it without that person's acquiescence to the act would be tantamount to cheating. But once Doug or Peter or Dave has offered the relief, taking it isn't cheating as far as our game and our round that day are concerned.

THE REAL VALUE OF GOLF: CAMARADERIE

We humans are social animals by our very nature: We interact continually with each other at home, at work, at play, on errands, when we're with friends. The great value of golf is that it gives people a reason for getting together. And as noted earlier, golf is virtually unique among all sports because people of widely varying skill levels can play it side by side. I know I've met and made some of my best friends as a direct result of golf. Many others have reported the same experience. My friendship with Doug, Dave, and Peter is a perfect example of what golf is really all about—providing the background for social interaction, the making of friends, and enjoying time together with a common interest. That's what's truly important.

Golf Etiquette for Golf Success

Etiquette matters. Golf etiquette matters. With it, you can navigate the minefield of decisions you have to make that aren't bound by the USGA's *The Rules of Golf*, but which will either impress or frustrate the golfers you are playing with as well as other golfers nearby. Embrace golf etiquette so that you can be the golfer who not only plays his best, but is also genuinely appreciated on the course and in the clubhouse. We all want to be the best golfer we can be, and one day I may get to a 10 handicap. But in the meantime, I have my 17-handicap game, which gets me around. Even more important, I have my friends. And they are the reason I keep going back. Sure, I want to improve my golf game—but really I want to hear that next story or that latest joke, or simply enjoy the beauty of the course and the experience of playing a terrific sport with people who matter to me.

The rest is simply icing on the cake.

tempers of golfers (*continued*)
  and sportsmanship, 5
  survey respondents on, xiv,
    122–23
thirty-yard rule, 50
throwing clubs, 130–31
Time, 158
tipping, 20, 52, 55–56, 180, 181
tobacco, 16, 144–45
tournament play
  and cheating, 117, 119
  conduct during, 148–56
  and flagstick rules, 98–99
  friendly play contrasted with, xv
  and hitting into other groups, 87
  and lost balls, 21, 72
  and playing through, 65
  and practice areas, 175
  and putting etiquette, 105
  and sandbagging, 120–21, 155
  and spectators, 140–47
  and twelve-minute rule, 80
TPC Scottsdale Stadium Course,
    145–46
tradition, 10–11, 26–28, 35
traps. *See* sand traps
Trevino, Lee, 158
trust, 8
twelve-minute rule, 80
two-putt rule, 65
twosomes, 23–24

United States Golf Association, xii,
    12–13, 44, 183, 191
urination, 18–19
U.S. Open, 1–2
USA Today, 108

wagering
  acceptability of, 169–70
  and alcohol, 19, 179–80
  game formats, 163–69
  guidelines for, 158–59
  and handicaps, 159–60, 160–61
  match vs. stroke play, 162–63
  and the nineteenth hole, 177–78,
    179–80
  paying bets, xv, 179–80
  and social element of golf, 157
  and temper of golfers, 127
waitstaff, 181
walking carts, xiv, 44–45, 47, 52–53
weather, 34, 102
Westchester Country Club, 80
wolf wager format, 168–69
women golfers, 14, 29–31, 85
Woods, Tiger, 61, 83–84, 97
Worcester Country Club, 1–2

the "X" rule, 58–59, 78

"yipping," 133

EMILY POST

JAMES MONTGOMERY FLAGG

EMILY POST, 1873–1960

Emily Post began her career as a writer at the age of thirty-one. Her romantic stories of European and American society were serialized in *Vanity Fair*, *Collier's*, *McCall's*, and other popular magazines. Many were also successfully published in book form.

Upon its publication in 1922, her book, *Etiquette*, topped the nonfiction bestseller list, and the phrase "according to Emily Post" soon entered our language as the last word on the subject of social conduct. Mrs. Post, who as a girl had been told that well-bred women should not work, was suddenly a pioneering American woman. Her numerous books, a syndicated newspaper column, and a regular network radio program made Emily Post a figure of national stature and importance throughout the rest of her life.

"Good manners reflect something from inside—an innate sense of consideration for others and respect for self."

—Emily Post

THE EMILY POST INSTITUTE

Emily Post has defined etiquette in America since 1922. Today at The Emily Post Institute, the third and fourth generations of Emily Post's family offer etiquette advice for the twenty-first-century.

The Emily Post library includes more than eighteen books on topics including everyday etiquette, wedding etiquette, business etiquette, and manners for children. In addition, the Posts author columns that appear in *The Boston Globe* (distributed by the New York Times Syndicate), *Good Housekeeping*, *Parents*, *InStyle Weddings*, *USA Weekend* and WeddingChannel.com.

The Emily Post Institute also offers a business etiquette seminar program, in which the Posts give seminars to Fortune 500 companies across the country as well as internationally. Representatives from corporations and individuals can also be trained through the Institute's "Train the Trainer" program, in which participants learn to teach children's manners classes or business etiquette seminars.

The Posts are quoted in hundreds of media interviews each year, including television, newspaper, radio, and magazine features that show how etiquette touches all aspects of life.

The Posts are available for public and private appearances, seminars, workshops, media interviews, and corporate spokesperson campaigns.

PETER POST

Peter Post is one of Emily Post's four great-grandchildren. As a director of The Emily Post Institute, Peter writes extensively about etiquette in America. He is the author of the *New York Times* bestseller *Essential Manners for Men* and *Essential Manners for Couples.* He also coauthored *The Etiquette Advantage in Business* with his sister-in-law Peggy Post.

Peter travels widely to present business etiquette seminars nationally and abroad. He also gives speeches to companies, organizations, and government agencies on general etiquette topics as well as on business etiquette.

For more information, please visit The Emily Post Institute at www.emilypost.com or call 802-860-1814.

ALSO BY PETER POST

EMILY POST'S THE ETIQUETTE ADVANTAGE IN BUSINESS
Personal Skills for Professional Success

ISBN 978-0-06-076002-1 (hardcover)

In this completely revised and updated edition, which includes three new chapters on ethics, table manners, and electronic communication, the Posts show you how to handle both everyday and unusual situations that are essential to professional and personal success.

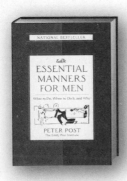

ESSENTIAL MANNERS FOR MEN
What to Do, When to Do It, and Why

ISBN 978-0-06-053980-1 (hardcover)

Peter Post, great-grandson of Emily Post, distills the essential information men need for all the important roles they play in life. Organized into three parts—"Daily Life," "Social Life," and "On the Job"—the *New York Times* bestseller *Essential Manners for Men* resolves situations that can stump even the savviest. Peter Post's advice is sharp-witted and sensible, with tips, boxes, and candid anecdotes about his own etiquette blunders. Short and shoot-from-the-hip honest, this is a book no man can afford to be without.

ESSENTIAL MANNERS FOR COUPLES
From Snoring and Sex to Finances and Fighting Fair— What Works, What Doesn't, and Why

ISBN 978-0-06-077665-7 (hardcover)

From the man who closed the lid forever on the "toilet seat debate" in *Essential Manners for Men* comes the follow-up book that paves the way for couples everywhere to fix relationship problems before they start. Peter Post offers the secrets to a long and happy marriage or partnership— without psychoanalysis or prescription medication.

COLLINS LIVING

An Imprint of HarperCollins*Publishers*
www.harpercollins.com

Available wherever books are sold, or call 1-800-331-3761 to order.